Stories For The Business Mind

JULIE-ANN BLACKMORE

DEDICATION

To all of my fellow travellers in the world of self-development, now, in the past, and in the future.
May we all live long, healthy, and prosperous lives and share our good fortune with others who are less fortunate..

CONTENTS

MORE WORKS BY JULIE-ANN BLACKMORE

INTRODUCTION

Welcome to this, my first book where business meets life and vice versa. this isn't the first book that I've ever written. It is however, the first book that I have written with only business people in mind. Most of my books have focussed on *how to be you* rather than how to be in business. It doesn't matter though for it's the same thing. You'll find out exactly what I mean by that as you read on.

With regards to the title of this book you will probably notice whilst you are reading this it seems to be void of stories. In fact there probably aren't going to be any in it. I don't know though until I write it, so this could all change at the drop of a hat.

Have I led you here under false pretences? Oh most definitely. But then haven't you?

Haven't you picked up this book for one reason yet really you know it's for another? Or rather you will when you have finished reading it. Didn't you pick up this book thinking that by reading stories you would be able to satisfy your business brain and learn a new way of thinking and working?

I can certainly guarantee you will get the end result it just might not come in the way that you thought or envisioned it coming. Or there again it might. Who knows? Only you as you read this book because you are the one who is reading it not me. I am simply writing it for you to learn whatever it is you think you need to know from choosing this book as your reading companion. I will teach you all that I know, and I will teach it over and over again in lots of different ways and on many different levels for your minds understanding. The one thing I will teach you is how to be you, by teaching you how to be me.

Sounds rather strange doesn't it? How could finding out how to be me teach you how to be you, let alone help you to have a more effective business?

Well, you are just going to have to wait and see on that one. So without further ado I give you the book that will not only change your life, your wife, your husband, your friends, your family, and you, but your business and career as well. I give you:

Stories For The Business Mind.

Why thank you. It's so lovely to be here speaking with you. We're going to have some fun here tonight. A lot of listening and learning will be going on. A lot of team building and finding out all of your own individual skills and talents as well. So that will be fun.

Okay then, where do we start I have so much to tell you?

I'm not sure. Oh, I know I'll start at the beginning where it all began. I'm not talking about the birds and the bees or God or the big bang. I'm talking about where it all began in **you.** How did you get to where you are now? Are you happy here, or do you just think or convince yourself that you are? Is your business mind being used to its full potential or are you holding back for fear of stepping on someone's toes? Are you really doing the job that you enjoy the most out of all jobs in the world or is there one out there that is better and perfect for who you are? Do you even really know who you are? These questions and many like them that I will make up as I go along will be answered throughout this journey.

For that is what this is, a journey about me for you to be able to help you find you and the right way of doing business for you. Or in simple terms it's a journey for you to be you. For when you are being you then the rest falls into place. A bit like a giant puzzle of life. You are the missing piece. Well not anymore you aren't, or at least you won't be after you have read this book. You will either love it or hate it. Then, you either love or hate yourself, so no change there. Or do you? Do you really know who you are well enough to form an opinion of like, love, dislike or hate on yourself or anyone else for that matter?

Do you really know who that person you sit by in your office is or are you merely guessing who they are by their clothes, their voice, and their mannerisms? Have you formed an opinion of yourself or others by your outward appearance? Have you even formed an opinion about your business on what it looks like from the outside? Have you even bothered to look below the surface and explore what

3

lies beneath? Well, this book will take you there. It will take you, if you are willing to go, and you always have the choice of whether you are willing or not, to the depths of your mind and beyond. It will take you on a tour of your business brain, opening doors and avenues you just didn't know even existed, and then it will land you safely back to where it all started, back to you.

Because that is where it does all really start and finish. With you and no one else.

Nobody can make you do anything or be anyone you don't want to be. You are who you are and that is why you are here regardless of what other people may think or create for you. As long as you remember that, as you read this book, then you will do fine and so will your business. In fact, you and your business and anything you choose to touch will do more than fine. It, and you, will always succeed. Failure will never be an option again. In fact the word just won't exist in your vocabulary. And this won't come about by hard work. No, this comes about by one simple thing that you have to do and keep doing; Be You.

That's as simple as it is. Now read on to find out how easy it is to do that and to encourage your business brain to take a hike so that you can get on with what you know the most about. Being you and living a life of pure enjoyment. This doesn't mean you won't get anything done. On the contrary you will become and stay more productive than you have ever been in your life. What it does mean is that you will not be working in vain or for another or in the way another says, and your returns will increase tenfold.

Sound good, or even too good to be true? Then read on

and find out how.

1 THREE STEPS TO A GOOD LIFE AND A GOOD BUSINESS

There are only three steps to a good life and a good business, and they are the following:

1. **Know Who You Are.**

2. **Know Why You Are Here**

3. **Know What You Are Supposed To Do Now You Know Who You Are and Why You Are Here**

That's it, do all of those and you are guaranteed an amazing abundantly happy life and business if that's how you've decided to apply them. To some, these steps may seem the simplest in the world. And some of you may be half way or all the way there. Well congratulations because even though simple as they are, they are no mean feat. In fact they are not mean at all, rather being very kind and easy to follow.

Others of you may be thinking, that there is no way you could ever do them, and I may as well be telling you to climb Mount Everest on one foot and your hands tied behind your back. Believe me they are extremely simple. You don't just have to believe me why not live them and find out for yourself how rich your life and business is?

Let's get some clarity on each step by breaking them down one by one and taking a more in-depth view of what I mean.

Step One: Know Who you Are

In other words know yourself. Not until you really know who you are can you start to live the life that you think you want to and know you deserve to. Only when you have the clear picture of yourself can you then be yourself.

So how do you do this? Do you spend lots of money delving into each crevice of your mind, and believe me that could go on forever as for every time you look inside your mind you can find a new crevice to explore? Or do you believe what someone else has written? Or do you listen to yourself and know your own truth about who you are?

Well, you can do all of these. You can spend years in therapy and counselling trying to work out who you are. Or I can tell you now, although you might not believe it yet or ever and that is your choice today. It may not be your choice tomorrow. If it's your choice today then that's good enough. Not good enough for a complete life of joy and abundance. Still good enough for you? Or you can go away on a retreat, learn to meditate, or take up any wonderful and eye-opening practice that will help you uncover whom you are.

Here's my short cut.

I spent months writing and living every word in nineteen books, including this one to find out exactly who I am, where I have come from as a human being and what I am supposed to do now I'm here. The one reason I did this was the reason why I am here. To share what I know with other people just like you so that you don't have to go through the pains and fears that my journey uncovered and created for me. So that you can take this insight as a short cut straight to a life and business or job or whatever you want without the unnecessary fear and pain we as humans seem to like to put ourselves under.

Interested? Then read on.

Bear in mind that anything I have written will only be understood by you at the level that your mind is ready to accept today, and that is fine today. You always have a choice, and you always will. You can choose to continue to read this book and find out about life and how you live it. Or you can choose not to. If you think that your way of living or doing business is great and working for you then that's fine by me. I really have no other interest than sharing what I know to be true to help people to live and work better. This way slowly the country, the nation and the world will change and become a lot more productive, affluent, and happy.

Now money alone doesn't bring happiness, but the thought of having it does. But what if you take that thought away. What then? What are you left with?

Actually, you are left with you. Pure and simple, you, with no thoughts. And that's who you really are. You are, as we all are, simply a channel for light, love, healing, and abundance whatever you want to call it. That's what you are. Get your head, your mind, and your thoughts out of the way and you as a person don't exist. You are merely a physical body filled with energy that is connected by a channel or tunnel to all the rest of the energy.

Now, if this seems a little too heavy going and spiritual, then that's fine. I did tell you it was a short cut to the truth. You will only believe what you want. If you still need to think things over and cause yourself more pain and chaos then you will. That's your choice and not mine. My choice is to merely offer you a different way of thinking until you realise that when you stop thinking, then you become who you are. And when that happens then life is sheer bliss. It is easy, fun, and full of gifts of love.

And love comes in many forms, depending on how you want it. It can come by gifts of money, or clients, or a partner or a new house. Whatever you want, when you recognise that you are actually connected to it energetically anyway, you can and will have it. There's no great debate. That is it. You are connected to all by this tunnel that goes up from your physical body and is always clear for you to channel light, love, wisdom, music, advice. Whatever your particular gift is, it will be flowing.

The only problem, and it's only slight, and it's You. Or rather not you, more your mind and the way you think. Because you insist on thinking and thinking and thinking and creating what you want with pain or pressure, stress, resistance, or hardship. That is what you get. You end up

9

blocking the channel to the true meaning of you and why you are here and how you can have all that you want by wanting it too much.

Imagine you are out for a walk. You notice an animal and want to take a closer look. You start to approach the animal but as soon as it sees you it starts to move away. You become more curious and more needy to see the animal, so you start to move in closer and closer. Meanwhile the animal isn't ready to have anyone close to it and moves further and further away. A chase eventually ensues. Now two things could happen. You may never catch the animal and give up, tail between your legs, and really fed up and tired. Or you catch the animal at what price? How is your health? Were you fit enough to run and chase it? Did you encounter unnecessary stress and pain on your chase or was it plain sailing? Did the animal bite you when you caught it because it wasn't ready to be caught or did you mishandle it and dropped it by mistake?

Now think of the same scenario, you are out walking, and you spot an animal you want to look at. This time you notice the animal and it notices you. You wait for it to approach you. And sure enough when it is ready it will come over and greet you. If you are kind and even more patient it may let you pet it and even pick it up. You may even be able to take it home and have it as your pet if you want to.

Now the end result was very different to the last. You didn't *persist* in wanting, you just waited patiently. The animal didn't *resist* in coming near it came over when the time was right. No broken or chewed fingers, no unhappy you or animal, no feelings of failure or stress, or pressure to succeed. Just an end result with no real effort on your part, and you still got what you wanted.

Now apply this to your life, either home life, personal life, business life or career or even the actual business corporation you work in. How much easier would life be all around, not only for you, for your friends and families and clients and colleagues if you adopted this new way of thinking?

There would be no comparison to how it is now. Would there? So if you can get the end result with little or no effort then why do you still need to try and try and try over and over again, chasing your goal further and further away from you?

Why? Because you don't know who you are.

Go back to work or to your partner or your family and friends and just for a small amount of time imagine that what I have said is true. How would this fact really alter the way you live your life, communicate with yourself and others and conduct business? How would what I have said open up your doors of possibilities and opportunities not for growth and change but for complete abundance?

When you fully accept that you are what I have said you are, merely a channel that is clear and able to pass free flowing energy of whatever you want it to be through you to others, then you get the life you want. I have accepted that I am a physical body attached to the whole of everything, a great pool of light and because my purpose is to bring light to others by words, I do. I am able to write this book and many others like it in less than two weeks. My gift to others and to myself is the gift of wisdom and love in the form of words either spoken or written. Your gift to others may be something completely different. Love and light comes in many guises. It can be in a beautiful piece of music or a wonderful poem. Or even in a passing smile. Love can be all around you and in you if you want it to be.

If this is now getting too airy fairy and elusive then don't worry. Again the idea is to open you up to new possibilities and ways of being, not to get you to join a cult or a convent. I am not a preacher of madness or religion. I only preach what I practice. If you really do want a life and business of abundance then take the first step and start to tell your mind that you are capable of anything and everything without effort. Of course your mind will wholeheartedly disagree and tell you a number of reasons why this isn't true. And that's fine for you today, and tomorrow is another day.

Tomorrow also never comes. Does that mean the choice does need to be made today? Do you choose to be you and have a peaceful, easy, fun, and extremely productive and wealthy life? Or do you choose to end up in more pain, stress, illness, and confusion?

The short cut to alleviate all of that is here waiting for you. All you have to do is take it. Take it and learn from it what you will. Uncover one more layer of truth for you, about you and let go of one more bunch of lies that your mind has been clouding your channel of light with. For that is what happens. Every time you think a bad thought, or a doubt, or say something negative then you automatically move further away from what you want to know, who you are and how you can have an amazing life, or business, or even be an amazing business as a collective.

For these steps will work in whatever way you apply them to whatever thing or person you decide to apply them to, as long as you have their permission. If you try to force your views, your business, your needs and wants onto another they will run just like the animal did. If you let them be and come to you then they will come bearing gifts of love and abundance.

For like attracts like and once you clear out your tunnel and recognise who you are, then you are able to truly receive the great gifts the world has to offer. Hence, you become affluent, happy, peaceful, loved, and loving. Whatever you want you get and with no real effort. Still sound too good to be true then that's just muddied your tunnel a little bit more.

What has?

That thought. Why? Because every thought that doesn't empower you as you, disempowers you and blocks your connection to all that you are and all that you can have.

So that's enough on step one, onto step two.

Step Two: Know Why You Are Here

This one's so easy it's almost laughable. When you've accepted and lived step one then step two is just a natural progression on from that. When you have caught the animal through kindness then it's time to accept why you have caught it. Maybe it needed to come over and be caught because it needed a new home, or maybe it needed some love, or maybe it just likes being petted. Whatever the reason the animal approached you. So now you know why you are here. Don't you?

No. Oh, why not?

I thought that because you are reading this you must be doing what you want to be doing otherwise why would you be reading a chapter entitled 'Three steps to a good life and a good business?' Well maybe the fact that you are reading this tells you already that it's time for a change in the way you are living or running your business whatever that may happen to be. Or you could do the first step and come back to this one later if you need to? But as I have already said when you really do accept and connect with your higher power, whatever name you wish to call it. You know step two inside out.

I only call your higher power a pool of light and love because my mind likes those terms. Other minds like God, or Higher Self or Soul or The One, The Source, whatever your mind will tell you what it wants you to be known as. All you really need to know is that if you are a free channel connected to this pool of whatever you call it, and we all are connected, then that means we all are connected. And that means we are all one. This then means we are all able to have the same gifts if we want. We can have infinite wisdom and knowledge. We can paint like the great artist Picasso if that is how we choose to live our life. We can write music like the astounding composer Bach, and you can write books like me.

It is no secret how I do this. I merely know who I am and that because of this, I let my energy flow freely from the light pit to me and out of me in the form of words, either written or spoken. That's it. No mystery and definitely no effort. I wrote this whilst I was in between things to do on a Saturday afternoon with no need to do anything other than write. I didn't spend hours slaving away before or after I wrote it trying to change it or edit it or telling myself it wasn't good enough. I merely let the energy in me bring the words and my mind read them as they appeared on the screen of my laptop. So not only am I the writer, but I am also the reader. There's a thought for you to mull over. How can I be the reader and the writer at the same time?

Simple, I do what I know I am here to do, and this is my gift for completing and living step one. What's yours? Have you found it yet or are you still searching? Well maybe this book will bring you a little closer to your truth and if not then hey, at least I've done my job for the day, and it only took me a couple of hours of pure bliss.

And so to step number three, I'm sure you've had enough of step two. And if you haven't then just remember one thing:

Any amount of searching will always bring you any amount of different answers. There will come a time when you just have to choose one and let it be.

Step Three: Know What You Are Supposed To Do Now You Know Who You Are And Why You Are Here?

Nothing

Absolutely nothing. And you can't get simpler than that.

What did you do to make the animal come to you? Nothing. What happened when you did do something? It ran away. And so it is with life and business. The more you do the worse it becomes. Give up fighting. Give in gracefully and be yourself. There really is nothing else for it. Once you have completed and lived step one and two then not only do you know who you are and why you are here, you also get what you are meant to get. Complete and utter abundance in every way you can imagine and more than a few that you can't even begin to think of.

Once you give up the ghost and clear your mind of past traits, problems, words, thoughts, issues, business deals gone wrong, mistakes and whatever then you become clear and pure to be able to just live the life you choose. You live life for you with love, happiness, and fun. You live in the way that you are here to live, and you become showered with gifts. People want to give you things. Opportunities that you could never imagine just drop straight into your lap. Clients phone you from out of the blue offering you major deals with no catch. Life does a 90° turn and so do you and your business, whatever that happens to be at the moment. Everything starts to change and get better. You ride on the wave of opportunity until you are ready to become that wave and bring opportunities to others.

For when you have completed and lived all three of the steps previously mentioned then you really do know how to be you and not only know it you are living, breathing, and enjoying it. I would even go as far to say that you are relishing in it and every moment becomes a moment of pure bliss. Happy to be alive, fulfilled and at peace with all that you know and all that you do and able to teach and help others to have a better life too. Just like I do.

So, please accept this gift of knowledge, wisdom, love, and light, whatever you want to call it. Remember it came from me to you, and only remember this because you know that if I can do it then you can too. I'll leave you with a little story for the business or inquisitive minds alike.

The Surfer, The Surf Board, The Teacher And The Wave.

Which one are you then? Are you perhaps the surfer that likes to look at the wave and then sits around waiting for it all day? Are you only able to enjoy the sport when the wave approaches? Always relying on something else creating this opportunity for fun.

Or are you the surfboard? You know that you have been the surfer and now you are willing to be the tool that the surfer uses to ride the waves of life?

Or are you, the teacher that teaches the surfer how to surf. You've been there, done it and brought the T-shirt so now you feel qualified to teach it. Or are you? Are you really qualified to teach what you know, or do you just think you are? Are you really teaching what you know or merely what someone else has told you to teach? Are you a free-flowing teacher or are you conditioned and rigid in your way of thinking? You decide on that one? I can't help you anymore. What I can do, however is teach you how to become the wave.

When you are the wave that is the fun part. You no longer need to wait around for opportunity to find you. You are the opportunity. You no longer need to ride the wave of life. You are the wave of life. You no longer need to teach in a rigid or inflexible, board like manner, you are your own teacher and as such can teach in the way that you really do know how to teach. Be that through words, pictures, movement, figures, stories, whatever is right for you will come down your channel as soon as you recognise yourself and let go of the rubbish that is currently blocking it up.

And how do you let go of all the rubbish?

Easy. You just stop thinking more rubbish for a start. Then you use whatever method you have available to you to learn how to ride the waves of opportunity. You make a commitment to be true to yourself and open yourself to allowing other waves to come into your life and offer their gifts of love to help you to change. You commit to being you and start to listen to the words of wisdom being fed your mind down your own tunnel of love. You commit to being you and you start living as you, for you. No longer following the crowd because you feel you have to. Rather letting others follow you if they choose to. You let go of the need to please others by what or who you are and just know that when you have accepted who you are then you can never offend or hurt another. It just isn't possible because you can only get pure energy down your tunnel. That is why my mind calls it light and love. Your mind may know it as something different. And that is why I know I am the wave, and you may not realise that you are too, with no more need to be the surfer.

I was the surfer and then I was the surfboard and then I was the teacher and now finally I am the wave. I no longer sit around waiting for opportunities to come my way to help me to grow. I am the opportunity. This book is your wave. Ride it on your board. Accept who you are and then let others see this and begin to accept you too. Once only the humble surfer who didn't know how to surf, then the teacher that taught the surfer, then the surfboard that needed no one to control it and finally the wave that controls nothing and everything by realizing my connection to all.

Your mind may like to call this egotistical and that is because you haven't let go of your mind. Let go of your mind and find out today the beauty that is in you and create the life you choose by doing absolutely nothing. Choose life and you and watch the seeds that you have been planting over time suddenly grow to fruition and be ready for harvesting. Don't worry about picking them yourself, let somebody else do that who still likes to do work the hard way by thinking too much. You sit back and reap the rewards.

The wave doesn't do anything to be a wave. It doesn't need to go anywhere or have anything or be anything other than a wave. Yet look at the power the wave has, the strength that it has to carry not only a surfboard and then a surfer on top of the board to the shore. Look how the wave just goes back and forth doing what it is here to do, minding its own business. Notice how the surfer seeks the wave out not the other way round. And why is this?

Because the surfer is dependent on the wave for their fun. The wave is not dependant on anything or anyone. It knows it is part of the ocean and if there were no waves then the ocean would be no more. You know that you are part of life and the universe and without you and lots of us, there would be no life or universe. Or if you don't know it yet, you will when you've completed the three steps to having that good life and good business you so badly want.

And not only is the surfer dependant on the wave for fun, but they also need the surfboard and if they don't want to teach themselves how to surf then they need a teacher. How complicated and needy is that? And probably unnecessarily expensive too.

Wouldn't you prefer to be the wave and be needy of no one and get everything you want?

I would and I am. That is why I have written this especially for you. So you can join me in this big ocean and recognise the power that you have in you and that you actually are the ocean and the wave.

And that is how you get a good life and business in three easy steps. In fact that is how you get everything that you have ever wanted. It really does just fall into your lap.

So, shall I lend you a broom to start sweeping out your channel of life or are you able to do it on your own. Do you need others to tell you how to run your life, your business and ultimately you? Or are you ready for the next step?

The end result.

I know I said there were only three steps to having a good

life and business. Then I also said that I was going to tell you a story and it turned out to be an analogy more than a story. I have no apology for you because that's just me exercising my poetic license and the genius in me decided to do it that way instead of the way you were expecting. Of course if I had let my mind get in the way then I would have got into a right state and ended up missing out the most important part, the end result. So thankfully, because I know and live the short cut, I didn't let my mind get in the way and I can continue down my path being me and not how others want me to be. This also means I can do what I want, say what I want, write what I want and know whole heartedly that whatever I do, say, or write will never be wrong. It might meet with some resistance on your part, but it will never be wrong on mine. And my life will never be wrong for me. I will never need to try to fit into someone else's shoes, or way of living or working. I can and always do live my life exactly as I please. With love and fun, happy, wealthy, healthy and with complete abundance in all ways. And all I have to do is be me.

That's the end result You not Me. Unless you still persist in resisting who you really

are, even after having read this article, I do find that hard to believe. But then I do find anything that I haven't written hard to believe because I do accept my way and it works for me. And whatever way is your way, then as long as it works for you today then that's fine for you.

And who knows about tomorrow. Maybe that will be the day your life changes and you start enjoying who and why you are and all of the wonderful benefits that brings to you, your business, the corporation or who or whatever you touch as a person. And that is what this is really all about:

How To Have A Good Life And Business.

Well isn't it?

Do you think there is more to life than having fun, enjoying yourself, bringing opportunities for others to grow, develop and change, living in abundance, happy and healthy. If you do then don't keep it to yourself share it. Maybe you've just discovered the real reason why you are who you are. Or maybe you just think you have?

I suppose the only way you can know for sure is give it a go. What's the worst that can happen? You find out how to have a good life and business? Come on, how bad can that really be? If it worked for me and we're all one of the same, then it can and will work for you. If you want it badly enough then you will stop wanting and learn acceptance and letting go and then you will have all you ever wanted. Whether you still want it when you get it is another matter, and indeed another chapter or book. For now I leave you with this tale of sorrow.

You, Your business, and Your Life, unless it's how you want it and then it's no longer a tale of sorrow but a tale of joy, happiness, affluence, and a tale of opportunity to help others know what you know. How to have a good life and business.

Goodbye and happy choosing which step to take first. Or maybe there are no steps left to take, maybe you have the end result, and you just don't know it. And that again my friend is a completely new chapter in the story of my life.

Could be that I will share it with you one day. Or perhaps you will never need to hear it, for you will be making up your own tales by then. Tales of when you were the surfer and how you got to be the wave and able to give to others what they need now, to grow and develop so they can also become the wave. Who knows? Only you do, not me. So stop reading and go out and see what life has to offer you. I can and will continue to write as long as I have surfers to ride on my wave of opportunity, I will be there. With no real beginning and no real end. Because that is how life is. You have only what you have now, so why not make that count and decide once and for all.

Are you the surfer, the surfboard, the teacher, or the wave?

Goodbye.

This chapter was written to be able to be applied to any and all walks of life. Be that in personal development, professional development or even as a corporation as the whole. You are the only one who knows how best to ride this wave of opportunity that you have already created to come into your life, and only you. After all, it's you who is looking for a good life and / or business, not me, I've already got it.

And that well and truly is the end result. And as you know results speak for themselves so don't just read about it, do it now

2 WHEN LIFE BECOMES WORK

What happens when your life becomes your work? No I haven't got it around the wrong way. I don't mean what happens when your work becomes your life. I mean it as I have first written it. What happens when your life becomes your work?

To some this sounds like an impossibility beyond belief as they never take their work home. To others it sounds like the worst thing that could ever happen to somebody. How could anybody want to live for a living? I'll explain that last question as you read on. And to others they know only too well the perils of your life becoming your work. Or do they? Do they really mean they know the perils of work becoming their life? I'm sure we've all been there at one time or another. You just don't have any time for fun or family or yourself because work is always getting in the way. Yeah, you know what I'm talking about. Having to get things done by a certain deadline either set by yourself or another. Waking up, with an active mind because you

24

have so much to do today and tomorrow. Endless sleepless nights worrying about working hard enough to pay the bills etc.

But do you know what it is like to live for a living? In other words do you know what it is like when your life becomes your work?

That's what I do,. I live my work. How? I'm a writer, speaker and teacher all rolled into one. I come under the name of Julie-Ann but what's in a name. Really I am just a channel for my amazing gifts of life. I went on a journey of life in which I uncovered layer upon layer of who I am. And now I know I suddenly realised why I am here to help others to live a good life and have a good business. And now I know who I am and why I am here then I can do what I'm supposed to do with this knowledge. And I do this by living my life for me.

I don't live my life for you anymore. I used to. I was the world's neediest, victim, people pleaser there was. What changed? Me. I changed because the people around me weren't going to change until I did. You only get what you want in this life. If you want hardship, pain and physical death of you, piece-by-piece and then that is what you will get. There will be lots of people to help you down that path. Telling you how to do things. Forcing you to go one more step to proof your worth or validation.

If, however, you decide to go down the other route and follow only one person, yourself. The real you that has been covered from the many layers and masks that you have hidden behind for so long, then your life becomes your work and that is no hardship. In fact it is so easy that

25

you will wake up one morning with an idea in your head, write it down within the hour, have it up and running within a couple of days and be reaping the rewards soon after that. With no pain, hardship, no change of character or personality. The end result, just you being you.

And by being you, genuinely who you are and living as you are supposed to, knowing your chosen specialities and gifts, and we have all got them. I don't know what yours are, maybe you do, or you don't. When you find out and accept who you really are under all your protection and memories of things gone wrong then you will know. And then when you do, you can really start to live your life.

For up until now I expect most of you are merely existing and not really living. Having the odd day or moment of fun, induced by some sort of stimulant, drug, person or event. And this is only existing. Living is when you are able to wake up with a smile on your face just because you are happy living. Living is when you are always at peace inside and enjoying life whatever or however you are living it, and with whom. Living is sharing in all of your beautiful gifts and talents without fear, just as the wave moving back and forth as part of the rich tapestry of life, the ocean. Living is working for pleasure and still living in complete financial abundance. And living is being able to let others live how they choose. No longer needing to fix or mend another or change their suggestion. Simply accepting that this is where they are today and that is fine by them, so it is fine to you.

People and businesses change at their own pace. And this is how it has to be. You cannot force something to grow or move or even listen. You have to be patient and like the animal before you, let it come to you. When it does then you will have no end of rewards. To force is to cause a resistance. There is a time for everything, and that time may not be now. When it is right, that is when it will come to you.

Foster patience within you and you will have the best skill in the world. And how do you have patience when you know there are bills to pay and a life out there to live? By exactly that. You live the life out there and in here that is waiting to be enjoyed. You live each moment as if it were your last and your first. This means you live each moment with eyes of a baby of awe of all the new wonders that surround you. And with eyes of a dying man that you might never get this one chance to see, feel or hear this again. You don't hold on; you just flow with it.

Have you ever had a time in your life when you were having so much fun, or you were so happy that it was scaring you? Maybe you had just cracked an amazing challenge or been offered the deal of a century at work. Everything was going just perfectly until this thought. "It's too good to be true, something bad has got to happen sooner or later." And sure enough it does. Why?

Because you ask it to. You lost faith in yourself and your abilities to be you and create the life you are creating because you got too happy. Is there some unwritten law that says, you must struggle hard all your life to earn money and then that will probably kill you? Or at least if that doesn't, the worry about how you are going to make more and more money will. And if that doesn't get you, then maybe the thought that it's all too good to be true will throw a spanner in the works so much that you lose everything, now that's got to hurt!

It doesn't have to be like that. Life can become your work, with ease, fun, love, time, wealth, and abundance as the end result. How? Well if you haven't already begun or finished the first three steps then may I suggest you at least start to explore what they might be like, and if you have, then may I suggest you stop reading this book and start writing your own. Or if you want to, may I suggest you stop listening to my suggestions and recheck whether you are actually being you, or are you still being who you think you should be.

You see we have two or more identities. Let's not make life any more complicated than I've already made it. So for now we will stick to just the two personalities.

Personality No. 1 - The Person You Think You Are

This is the person that wakes up in a cold sweat fretting over work or family or money or whatever. This person wakes up and needs to go for a run because either they are

a)   Worried about getting too overweight or unfit

b)   Following orders from another i.e. A doctor, the television set, or the back of a cereal packet.

c)   Goes off running because they are too scared to have any time to themselves when they might find out the truth about who they are and the way they live their life, or conduct their business

This person, after running and not really enjoying it, or telling themselves they have because they think it's good for them, then starts to get ready for work. This person is excited at going to the office or place of work, or is it really anxious that they should do a good job? Anyway, whatever, they go to work, maybe grabbing a coffee or breakfast on the way. This person gets to work, and the excitement soon changes to that anxiety I was talking about, as the pressure increases. The work load also increases and so does the person's stress and tension. This person usually works through lunch believing they can't take time out or has a drinking lunch to try to alleviate their stress and unwind.

The end of the day is nearing, and this person still has a massive pile of work to be done by tomorrow or sooner. So instead of leaving their work in the office where it should be, they bring it home. This person may need to go for another run or do some active exercise just to escape from the day before they finally get to sit down with friends, family or on their own. If on their own then they will carry on working where they left off. If with others they may over indulge in food or drink to numb the pain they feel inside or just to be sociable. This person goes to bed eventually exhausted and still with work on their mind. They get up the next day and it all starts over.

Now after a while this person may get ill from stress and overwork. They may go bankrupt or be financially

successful depending on how much their work means over their health. This person may end up becoming so like other people or who they think they should be, they just don't know who they are and constantly rely on others to help them forge their personality. This person may become more and more insecure in who they are and in their own wonderful talents and abilities that are hard to beat. This person may become so much like the person they think they are, that they never get to find out who they really are and live the life of the person below. And that is a crying shame. And it is.

This person probably is no stranger to crying or to shame or to therapy. This person has so much complication and torment in their life they will probably end up trying to sort it all out for years to come. Not to mention all the potions and medicines they may find themselves taking, again on the advice of another, prescribed or otherwise. This person may become so much like the person they think they are, that they start to believe it and actually don't like that person. Thus spending more money on ways of how not to be this person or how, worse still, to get to like this person. And that is where the problem lies. Why would you want to get to like or even love a person that is merely a figment of your imagination?

Because that is what this person really is, a person borne out of fear. Fear from not knowing who they are, or ever finding out who they are, or fear of not liking the real you. This person may be you. Let's hope for everyone's sake that it isn't, and you are more like the next person I am going to describe.

Personality No. 2 - The Real You

This person is completely different from the other one. Let me show you how.

Firstly this person gets up and goes to bed whenever they feel like it. Not worried about how much sleep they will or won't have because they know they always have enough, whether that is two or six hours. They always sleep well and never lay awake worrying about anything.

This person gets up taking their time. For that is one thing this person has, lots of time. Unlike the other personality this person does not need to put pressure on him or herself. They know there is a time for everything and everyone and that time will come more quickly and easily if you let it just appear. How does this person know that? Because it has happened, time and time again. So this person trusts and believes in their self to make things happen by not making things happen. This will become clearer later on.

This person may do some work before breakfast, whatever that is. Work to them is fun and always creative and full of inspiration. Just like their life. There is never a need or hurry to get things done; things just get done when they are supposed to. This person is extremely productive and that is why they can do what they want when they want to and still earn good money. This person enjoys running some days and others not. This person enjoys walking on long walks and other days not. Sometimes this person just wants to lounge around the house and other days they just want to get out and see the world.

Some days this person likes to be entirely on his or her own, quiet, and meditative, listening to music, working and being still. Other days they like to not work and go out and party all day and all night, without the aid of any drugs, stimulants, or alcohol. They just know each day is a party and the fun and enjoyment never ever stops. Some days this person likes to watch television or read a book and other days they don't, preferring to have no outside stimulus at all.

Some days this person is sad about what is happening in the world, but they are never in pain. This person doesn't believe in pain in their life and therefore doesn't need to create it for him or herself anymore. This person also knows that happiness is not something to hold but rather something to have and enjoy and let go of. Therefore this person is always happy. This person makes you sick, but never gets sick him or herself. This person doesn't need to follow the advice of others preferring to listen to their own body and feeding, resting, and exercising according to its needs and not someone else's. When I say this person makes you sick, I don't mean they do anything bad to you. In fact this person is one of the nicest loving people you would care to meet. Never hurting or harming another by their words or actions. Only offering gifts of love, happiness, abundance and more. What makes you sick is your envy. This person never has that problem either because they just don't feel jealous of anyone or judge anyone else. Why would they want or need to? They don't judge themselves anymore because they are happy being them and they love the life they lead so they don't want anybody else's. Therefore no need to be nasty or unkind about or to anyone.

Now this person is beginning to sound like a saint and an anomaly that doesn't exist. This is so far from the truth you wouldn't believe it until you become this person. Until you are the real you then you won't really know what I'm talking about, will you? And when you do, then you will. My God, you will. Oh yeah, this person doesn't follow any particular religion or belief system. In fact this person doesn't need to follow anyone preferring to follow his or her own words of wisdom rather than another. Everybody has their own way of being and that is right for them. Just because it's right for one doesn't mean it's right for all. And this person knows, understands, and lives this. That is why at the end of their day they have accomplished more today than the first person could in over a week, and they can go to bed knowing that life is amazing, and that work is amazing. They go to bed with no worries; in fact, they don't worry about anything anymore. What's the point? Worries only block reality and they love reality so much and all the joy, love, and abundance they have found and keep on getting why on earth would they want to?

And yes, in case you were wondering, they are of this earth. They recognise that just because they live here in a physical body, doesn't mean to say they are restricted to being here. So they are not. They choose to travel around the atmosphere and create all they want. How do they do that? They recognise that they are merely energy connected to all the rest of us who are energy as well. They lose the power of their mind and increase the power of their self. They choose to stop thinking thoughts that just get in the way of what is really going on and enjoy every moment of every day with awe and wonder as if it were their first and with love and excitement as if it were their last. They know that by living like this they will never have a last moment of happiness because every moment is happiness. They know that work will never go bad, be a bind or cause them fear because their life isn't like that. And they know that their life is their work, work, not in the sense of personality number 1's work. But work in the sense of it's what pays the bills. So in effect what really pays their bills is being true to themselves, by just being themselves and doing what they enjoy the most, which ultimately helps you.

And that's another thing this person doesn't need, help. Yet help arrives in the many different forms that it can. This person is always being offered wonderful gifts that ease their physical and material living and further their success. And all they have done to get their life like this is their self. First, you have to choose to be this way. And that is one thing that personality two does have over personality one, apart from all the other things previously mentioned, and that is choice. Personality number two always has choice. Choice of who they are, what they do, where they go, what they say, how they work etc. This personality really doesn't need others to tell them how to be or how to live, for this person has discovered their own unique way and is sticking with it. Yet they never get stuck. This person is constantly moving on and upwards in terms of success and growth in the eyes of personality number one. In the eyes of personality number two, they don't really change only the circumstances and people around them do. Like the wave this person, now they know who they are and how to be themselves, stays being like that for the rest of their life.

Does that sound boring to you? It may well do. It isn't though and that is one thing this person never gets is bored. How could they when

a) They live such a wonderful life

b) They live such a wonderful life

c) They live such a wonderful life

How could they ever get bored when their life is their work? They can't and they don't they just get happy, healthy, wealthy, and abundant and stay like that forever. On one condition, that they stay being themselves and do not go back to being personality number one. Otherwise the whole cycle of what they know starts over again and life is no longer their work. Life is once more a drag and something to be feared or ran from instead of loved and enjoyed.

So who are you?

Personality one who runs in fear of life and all it has to offer you?

Or

Personality two who runs for fun head first into the open mouth of abundance?

You decide and when you have worked out whether that was really your choice or someone else's, then decide if you like it that way or not.

If you do that is fine. There is no one forcing you to change unless deep down you are.

And if you don't then that's fine as well? Perhaps you would like to change it and step from personality number one into personality number two. Well, you know what you have to do, don't you?

Just Be You

Oh one more thing I forgot to mention about personality one.

They always follow somebody else's suggestions instead of their own. It doesn't matter how good they know theirs are, they still end up believing in another's to give them their new identity. What's wrong with their old identity? Well they are not really sure who they are anymore, lost in the sea of waves and opportunity. Instead of remembering, like personality two does, that they are the opportunity not the other way round. They can never get lost because they are the sea and the wave, so how could they? They just can't, it's as simple as that.

Be you and whatever happens or whoever comes along with their wonderful offers will never change whom you are or why you are here. And that means you will always have the life you want and the work you choose to do and enjoy. Otherwise, I personally can't think of any good reasons why I would work if not to enjoy myself. And the fact that I get paid for doing something that comes so easy to me is a bonus on top of the bonus of having lots of time to do everything else I love, on top of the bonus of loving everything I do. So you see by being personality two you really do have everything you want, and you give others what they want too. With no real effort, just you being you and leaving them to be who they are today.

Now you know personality two does exist and it isn't a figment of your imagination like personality one is. It is tangible and it is here guiding you through this book. So enjoy what you are beginning to create and live your work as only you know how, being you.

3 THOUGHT VERSUS REASON

What happens when thought versus reason? Aren't they really one of the same thing and we are just looking at them differently? Isn't that how we lead our lives? We think something is there for one reason and it turns out to be a completely different reason than we first thought. Does that mean that thought is going hand in hand with reason? Or that thought follows reason or vice versa? Or maybe thought versus reason as we once said? How could we know or ever find out?

We don't and we can't unless we do one thing. We let go of the need to think for a moment and let go of the need to reason and then see what we have. We see that nothing has changed. Nothing has changed around us or inside of us. The only thing that was creating this dilemma and this chapter was my mind. There is no difference between thought and reason they are completely one and the same.

How do I know this? Because I have just proved it. How have I proved it? By turning off my mind and seeing what was left. Nothing. Nothing apart from that and me is what was left.

And that is what is always left when you turn off your mind, You. Plain and simple, you. Although you or nobody else is just plain and simple. On the contrary you are a wonderful, fascinating, and very talented individual. You might not think it, and reason may tell you otherwise. But when you let go of all thoughts and reasons and you are left with just you, then you know what I am talking about. And I am talking. These books are speaking to me. That is my gift of being me. I learn by what I write, today and tomorrow and the next. Everything I am writing here, now, is not only relevant to you in your area of work, life, career, corporation or whatever. These words are also relevant in my line of work, living my life. We may be poles apart, yet what is good for you is even better for me, because not only do I write it, but I also get to learn from it by reading it and I haven't spent any money. In fact I'm getting paid to do this.

How good is that?

And your life can be this easy too? You can spend your days doing exactly what you want and reaping the rewards every which way you turn. And how do you do this?

By turning off reason and thought. In effect by losing your mind. Not going mad or anything so unsettling and traumatic as that. God no, I don't preach pain I only preach what I practice else how could I learn from my words and still enjoy my life? I couldn't. So rest assured whatever you think I'm preaching, be it religion, a marketing tool, a new way of life for everyone in the same way, I'm not. Whatever you think or reason I'm doing then you are wrong and always will be. If, on the other hand you are willing to let go of your reason and logical thinking for one moment, then you will know what I am talking about.

I'm talking about love, life, and the universe. I'm talking about how you, as you, can fit into the world doing what you want to and still run or work in a business you love. I'm talking about how you, being you, can go to work every day for somebody else and love every minute of it and still enjoy it in 50 years' time. I'm talking about you, as you, living the life you choose, with the people you choose doing the things you enjoy and forgetting the word work ever existed and still having money for all that you need or desire. I'm talking about one simple thing. You being you.

That's it. That is all this book will continually talk about to me and to you. It will offer you new and exciting ways of firstly thinking, and then teach you how to let go of those thoughts to allow the real truth about you to come in. I'm talking about the real you finding out exactly the reason why you are here without needing to think or reason it at all, just being it. I'm talking about an abundant life full of joy and freedom, doing everything you love the most in your world. I'm talking about….

I'm talking too much so why don't you do some talking now? Why don't you have a serious talk with personality number one and see if you can't try and convince them to be more like personality number two for a while? Why don't you do something you really enjoy and come back to this when you are good and ready? For one thing I have learnt on my travels into the depths of me, you can't force change. Why would you want to anyway? That would just mean you were getting more like personality number one again and you don't want that do you?

Or do you?

Do you still want to be like personality one and no longer live the life you choose to live? Ending up living for somebody else, working for somebody else and being like somebody else all in the name of fear? Or would you rather work for you, enjoying all you are and all you do. Working and living in the name of love?

The choice again and as always is yours. You decide and return when you are ready. Hopefully when reason and thought have gone and all that once again remains is you.

After all, you came into this world alone and you are certainly going to leave it alone so why would you need others to tell you how to run your life for you up until that point when you do leave? You wouldn't and you don't when thought no longer versus reason, and you realise they are just words in your head.

And words in your head can't hurt you. Only the thought or reason that you attach to them can. So why would you want to hurt yourself unless you were being personality number one instead of two. Beats me, but then lots of things have beaten me in the past. Beaten me into submission. And now I know better than to let my thoughts and reasons take over because they just spin me a tale so long and false that life just really does end up a pain. Not only a pain in the butt, but a pain in the soul as well.

For when you are being led by your head and not yourself

then it really is soul destroying. And we all know what that feels like. You know the feeling when you no longer know who you are or why you are doing what you are doing. You feel like a lost child in a desert of blowing sand. Not sure which way to turn next and waiting for someone to arrive to take you to freedom or home. But you are already home. You might not realise it yet, but you will. You have already taken the three steps to living your life as you, for you, doing what you do and loving every minute of it.

No?

Then go off and do that now and I'll be here waiting without reason and thought. And along with that goes doubt. For when you let go of thought and reason then all the doubts you've ever had, or can have, disappear. Gone without a trace just like that. In fact they disappear that quickly that you forget you ever had any and you just get on with doing what you know best, how to be you.

4 THE ORDER OF THE DAY

Good your back. I hope reason and thought haven't tripped you up too much. And if they did then don't worry I'm sure this chapter will sort you out and if this doesn't, then I don't know what will. Because all I do is what I do best, and this is write what I know and all I know is how to be me. So whatever I write, in whatever way I write it be it stories, poems, tales or fables, truth or fiction there is always the same message. I merely repackage it over and over and over and over again, until you have let go of all thought and reason and can stop reading it as your own. Because it isn't, it's mine. Your way could be and probably is completely different to mine.

My way has guided me from personality number one to personality number two. You see, I got fed up of being second best and split down the middle on all my decisions, so I just got rid of personality number one and am content being number two, which has now become the one and only me.

You on the other hand may still be looking for opportunities to come your way instead of realising you are the one creating them. You are the wave not the surfer, surfboard, or the teacher. You are the wave that creates your own way by being who you are and nobody else. There will always be somebody there to offer you an opportunity to grow and develop until you realise, finally, that you no longer need to. The wave doesn't change. It is always constant at being a wave. It's circumstances and position and how it creates opportunities for others changes and keeps on changing. The wave doesn't and neither does what controls it, the ocean. So remember you are the wave that makes up the ocean. You are not the boat that rides and tosses and turns on the wave when a storm comes. You are the storm. You don't get affected by the storm because you become part of it and helped to create it. You are it. This means that you never have turmoil or upset in your life ever again. That is unless you invite it in. And how do you stop doing that?

That is the order of the day:

Letter To Self

To be distributed to all relevant persons

Dear Personality Number One

It has come to our attention that you are not pulling your weight as you should be, and you are really creating chaos when you should be creating calm and peace. You have been found slacking off of work and constantly known to be complaining about the tasks that you have been given to do.

Unfortunately after due thought and consideration on your part and not ours, we have decided that the only way forward for us to survive and not only survive but grow and prosper is to recognise that this place isn't big enough for the both of us. So one of us has to go.

Now if we look at the pros and cons of you remaining then we will be overanalysing and creating more and more reasons and thoughts than we will have time to get through. If we look at the pros and cons of why I should stay then you will find none. Apart from one.

And that is it.

The sheer fact that there are no pros and cons is the only reason why I should stay, and you should go. How is that so, you may be asking yourself? And you can continue asking yourself until you are blue in the face or hell freezes over. You will be and it won't. You will be blue in the face. For as many reason and thoughts as you can think of you will be able to think of at least ten more and then ten more and then ten more. Until you are thinking for an eternity and hell will never freeze over so there's your reason for that.

Of course, whilst you have been doing all of this thinking nothing has been getting done. And most of all you haven't been enjoying yourself. And, that my friend is the worst crime of all. And you are my friend, even though you know what is coming next, you still are my friend. For without you I would not have been able to create all of the wonderful opportunities that I have to be able to get to this point today. And now, where does that point exist?

Here, right here, nowhere else. And that is another reason that there can only be one of us because beyond this point there can be no more thinking or reasoning, it just takes up too much valuable time called life. And as we've only got one or so you have heard others say, then I intend to live mine to the best of my ability. And that my friend is by being me and not you.

So it looks like you are going to have to go. But don't be sad or worried about me because I will be alright. You can guarantee that. Only you can't because you don't believe that that's why you have to reason or think about what is going on or going to happen. And that, again my friend, is another reason why you just can't stay. If you need any more reasons then I'm sure you can come up with them yourself and I'll leave you to do that while I do the most important thing that we came here to do:

Live.

So I'll love you and leave you. Because when you get rid of all thought and reason all that is left is really only you. And you really are only love, there is nothing else. And love attracts love in many different ways and love comes in many different forms, as you are about to find out. Or rather you won't if you don't let me go and be personality two instead of one all the time. After all it's up to you not me. I've brought you this far and can take you no further the rest is up to you. Personality number two or are you still happy being second best?

I'm not so I'm off to be me. Who are you off to be, one or two? Come join me if you like, it's up to you. Be glad of the choice whilst you still have it, because soon enough you won't. If you persist in thinking then you will keep on believing you are everything but the wave. That means you will always be faced with opportunities to grow and change and will miss out on all the lovely abundance that you will have by giving others the opportunities to grow and change. And that would be a terrible crime.

So I leave you with these kind words. I love you and you have really helped me to the door of my life. Now somebody has opened it, and I must walk inside and leave you behind. There are no hard feelings and there never will be. This is just the way it is and was always going to be, otherwise why would I have found a book telling me how to be you. I know who you are, and I don't want to be you anymore I want to be me. I need to be me and stop needing and just be. So this is where we part company, me to be me, and you to be you somewhere else instead. I know lots of people who would love to have you stay with them for a while longer, but I don't, so this is it. I'm off now. Thank you for your kind thoughts and reasoning. I'm pretty sure that I wouldn't have got to where I am today without all your interventions. Who knows maybe I would have found this place a lot sooner but what has happened has happened and I do not hold regrets I only have complete gratitude in you.

Once again I thank you and say if there is anything you need then stick around and watch it roll in. For anything you've ever dreamt or desired is just on the horizon and will only come over if you go. Sorry, you can't really stick around but at least you are going, safe in the knowledge that your role has been worthwhile. After all you were only here to protect me and make sure I was happy. And now I am you can go.

So, goodbye, and good luck being you, whoever you are, because you never were really sure of your own identity were you? It must have been hard for you knowing that you could have been me but not really sure how to be because you kept listening to everyone except who you should have been listening to. Me. Oh well, never mind, past is past and all we have is the present. Or rather all I have is the present and how wonderful is that, and what more could I honestly ask for? Knowing I am safe in the hands of the universe. That I have the knowledge and wisdom of the universe at my fingertips and that I have the love and kindness of a thousand gurus in my heart. And of course, what you have always been concerned with and thought made the world go round, money. Although that isn't what makes the world go round, I am. But that isn't important to me, and neither is money nor never will be. And because it isn't important I will always have plenty. 'My cup runneth over as they say.' Who says, I don't know, the fact that I know it is enough for me, not for you though. Nothing, including me was ever good enough for you. You always wanted more and more and more. Never content with what you have now, always thinking or worrying about what hadn't or had happened. Well no more my friend, only this moment is the most important moment this one and no other. For there is no other, and again why would you want there to be?

Well, you would, and I don't, so it really is time to terminate your employment in this space. Thank you once more for all your hard work because I know how much you have valued yourself on the job you have done, or on the response from others you have received. So I will once again say thank you, and again and again and hope that you now understand and have enough reasons to know the truth.

There is no longer room for you.

So, one more thank you so as not to dent your pride and I will be gone. Goodbye and take care. I don't need to hear that because I know it. There is only abundance in my life nothing more and nothing less. That means no fear, no lies, no cheating, no validating, no remorse, no more opportunities to change who I am and no more restriction or resistance. Just abundance.

So, why would I want to change that?

I wouldn't, I don't, and I am definitely not going to. I know I can't change you because that is part of being me; I can't change another or force them into my way of being. Not that I'd want to anyway, I have no pride or ego to dent. I'm just me and that really is enough.

Of course I'm not really going anywhere, you are.

Please collect your thoughts and leave with them by the end of this working day.

If you have any problems with this then we will have to evict you from this building never to darken my doorstep again. I hope that you can go in peace, as it is better for all those concerned.

Yours Forever True, Personality Number Two

5 SIGNS AND SYMBOLS TO SUCCESS

I don't normally talk about my own personal experiences as they are happening, any more. Although I did right up until I started writing this book and the letter to Self. You see I couldn't see. I couldn't see that I was still being personality number one and being second best to who I was. I was constantly reinforcing this idea by the opportunities for growth that I kept creating into my life and by openly admitting that I was not only the writer but the reader of my work as well.

So who was really writing it?

Me all along, personality number two. Personality number one, the doubter, the one that hadn't accepted who I really was and am now and actually always have been, was reading it. Not only was I reading it, but I was also living it and I was not enjoying it because I was constantly being faced with opportunities for change and no abundance. Why would I want to change if I knew who I was and had done all the developing I needed to?

An adult doesn't keep on physically growing after they have been through puberty. We don't suddenly get much bigger breasts, unfortunately, or more hair, fortunately. Our hair does grow, and our breasts change in shape and size depending on our circumstances, but they don't change what they are. Probably not a very good example to use particularly for all you men out there. And that is what happens when you try to please other people and not yourself. You end up making a hash, a mess of things, doubting yourself, repeating words you've already written and going over and over the same thing.

Puberty happens only once, and this is your opportunity for it to happen to you. Puberty of the business mind. Not mine though because my puberty happened and was over a long time ago, I just didn't realise it. It didn't matter how many times I read the words I was writing I still couldn't really let go of personality number one. For one, I didn't really know I had one. And that is the problem. They, you, are very crafty, and believe me you can have more than one personality. You can have any number of personalities working for you in your head. This isn't to say you have schizophrenia, although the word only refers to having more than one identity, so I suppose you could say we are all schizophrenic until we sort out who we are. Now, before you go rushing off to the nearest psychiatrist or therapist who will accommodate you by confirming your suspicions, let me tell you a story. Yes, now I'm going to tell you all a story. Mind you, I'm not going to tell it to myself because this one is about me:

The Story Of Me

Brought up in a loving and caring environment, if somewhat over protective I didn't really have a very happy childhood. It wasn't because of anything that anyone had done; rather it was something that I had done or hadn't done to be precise. It was because I had failed over and over to recognise who I really was and the gifts that I can bring to others who want them.

All the signs were there and kept on coming but I didn't. Instead I kept on going. Moving further and further away from who I am today, preferring rather than listening to my own voice, to anyone else who would speak to me.

I wasn't very popular in school. In fact I was hated in school. Hated is too strong a word. No hated is the right word because it was me that did the hating of me. I really did hate myself, or who I thought I was. And that was my problem, I thought too much. I had an extremely analytical brain, a bit like my fathers who is an engineer, but I'm not an engineer. I didn't need an analytical brain for what I can do.

As I got older I realised that I had the power of second sight. I could see, feel, hear, and smell things other people couldn't, or wouldn't admit to anyway. I used to ignore it for fear of becoming an outcast to society. I was hated enough, remember, I didn't want to give myself any more reasons for hating myself. Or did I?

Yes, unfortunately, or fortunately depending on which way you look at it, I did. So I did. I gave myself lots and lots of reasons why I could continue to hate myself. The main one being I was never good enough and would never amount to much. I really had lost my way, or so I thought.

You see I hadn't, and we never do lose our way or our identity we just think we do.

Time went on and I became excellent at giving words of wisdom in the cloakrooms to my friends and school colleagues at lunchtime. (Yeah I know I said I was hated, but it turned out all to be in my mind. I told you I thought and analysed far too much.) More time passed and I joined the Red Cross Society to begin following my passion to be a nurse. Only what I really enjoyed about the courses I attended, and the competitions was that I could lead people into success, and I could help people who were in pain.

More time passed and eventually I left school and got a job doing something that I thought was me but wasn't really. How do I know? Because I don't do it anymore that's how. There was a brief period in between that and being accepted for nursing where I was depressed. Not unhappy, I was completely depressed, body, mind, and spirit. Not sure why at the time and now I know. I had almost tarred and feathered myself so much with my own hatred I had completely lost my identity and purpose for being alive. So in that case what was the point in being alive? Not sure again at the time, but I was determined to find out. And bit-by-bit I did.

I became a nurse and loved every moment of it. The hustle and bustle, I had become a bit of an adrenalin junkie, due to the fact I was always on fight or flight because I was always fighting myself. Part of me was telling me how wonderful, loving, kind, an excellent leader and healer I was. Whilst the other part was reminding me how terrible I was, that I would never be enough and never amount to anything at all. This internal struggle went on for a long time until suddenly and without surprise because this is eventually what happens, it became external. I was lucky it didn't kill me as in some people. I just had a car crash which set me back a few years and gave me a lot of physical pain and restriction to match the mental torment I had put myself under.

Actually the car crash didn't put me back at all it brought me forward. Kicking and screaming into the reality of that which I am. The person who now stands before you. The leader, the healer, the guide, and advisor. Whatever you want to call me it doesn't matter. What does matter is that I am me.

After years of struggling to find me, I was being me all of the time. I even had a tattoo of the Egyptian symbol of the Eye Of Horus on my thigh and this later became my business symbol with the name 2ndsight coaching. I worked as a psychic life coach. But that isn't who I am. The symbol represents one of my gifts although I didn't realise it at the time to its full extent. It stands for the all-seeing, all-knowing eye. The god Horus represents truth, insight, wisdom, and inner knowledge. Protection and fertility. And that is who I am

A few years later when I had completely cured myself of the physical pain I had four symbols tattooed at the base of my spine. I decided on the particular designs for one reason, which actually satisfied my personality number one until now when I know the truth. And the truth is the symbols represent who I am and always have been.

I have Meretseger, the sign of a snake, who is another

Egyptian god. She is a powerful healer and doesn't suffer fools gladly, as you will know if you have read another of my books Inspirational Words For An Inspirational World. She also helps others who want to be helped and always shows respect for them and herself. She often takes time to step back and reflect on the choices she has made ensuring she is doing them for the right reasons. In other words in the name of love and not fear.

The next two symbols are the Chinese symbols for the word freedom. I thought I was getting these to remind me of the pain I had cured in my back from the car crash. Now I know different. I am freedom. I am freedom and I bring freedom to others. Freedom from the fool, which lies within us all. Freedom, from personality number one so we may be personality number two. And freedom for me to be me and you to be you. The last and most beautiful symbol is the Chinese word for love. I knew why I was getting this because after all that is all we are. But it wasn't until today that I really experienced that knowing. I am only love and bring love to others in many ways, by the touch of my hand, by the sound of my voice, by the words that I write or say.

I also have two other symbols on my body. I thought they were meaningless, and I only had them done for something to do and to offend my parents. They are two Chinese dragons and both of them are breathing fire. And that is what I do. I breathe fire at you so that you may burn your rubbish with my words and my love for you. You are like the moth that comes too close to the flame. I am the flame that singes you and keeps on burning you every time you come back for more, which you inevitably do. Why? Why does a moth keep going to the flame even when it knows it will be burnt and eventually die? Why, because it is attracted by the light. And that is what makes you come back for more and more until you are the flame and others come to you to be burned.

So, now you know the ins and outs of who I am. Who are you?

I'll leave you to ponder over that one. Or maybe you no longer need too because personality number two already knows who they are. Don't you?

Maybe you have got some tattoos or symbols on or around you that are really big clues as to who you really are and why you have come here. When you find them and interpret and understand their truth, then you can once more recognise and be you.

This can also apply to the company or area of work you are in. Has the true meaning of that become tarred and feathered by yours or other judgements as to what it is all about? Or is the purpose clear? Maybe it isn't as you and your colleagues once thought? As you all start to become more aware of yourselves as whom you really are then the true identity of your business or corporation will also start to be uncovered for you.

Remember nothing really changes only your perception of it changes. My tattoos haven't changed, only the meaning I put behind them has. And this is how it is in life, be it personal or professional. You don't really change only your perception does. You don't have to change. What needs to change is your split personality once and for all. You need to put yourself first and get rid of being second best all together, otherwise somebody will come and burn you all up. And believe me that hurts. You think this book is close to the knuckle then you want to have written, read and lived the seven that came before and the many afterwards. Not a pretty sight. Although they were and always have been, and so am I, I just couldn't see it for personality number one obscuring my view all the time.

So, do whatever it takes before you move onto the next chapter to remove personality number one from your building and return whole being you and only you. As always I'll be here until you're not.

6 TO APPROACH OR NOT TO APPROACH?

Welcome back number two, good to see you going it alone at last!

Anyway, now you're here and all ears let's get down to business. Why are you reading a book entitled Stories For Business? What do you think that I can tell you or offer you that you haven't already offered yourself? It's interesting really how many people rely on others to tell them exactly what they already know. Isn't it? I find it interesting. I suppose that's the way of the world. The business world anyway, if not your own life as well.

If you were to take a look around you at your business environment and study what everyone is doing and ask them why, how many people would say, "Because so and so told me to." Or "That's the way we've always done it isn't it?" The last part comes from the question, "Why...." because you have instilled some doubt into that person's mind as to whether they really should be doing it or not.

Or have you really instilled doubt in that other person's mind or was it there anyway? How many people are doing something, and this could include you, just because it is the way it has always been done? If it isn't broken then don't fix it, mentality. Now there is nothing wrong with this way of thinking, unless and this is a big point so listen and read carefully. Unless you and the people you work for, or with or even employ don't actually notice that it is broken and has been for a long time. In fact it has become so broken it has been held together with vinegar and brown paper, like in the nursery rhyme of Jack and Jill who went up the hill. Jack fell down and Jill came tumbling after. Is that what is happening to you and your company or corporation? Are you climbing the hill only to find that one of you trips and falls? Probably tripped up by reason or thought alone could do it. And then you all go tumbling after. Are you the one who has led the falling brigade and has to have your head bandaged with vinegar and brown paper? Or are you the one that has realised that it is broken and vinegar and brown paper and any amount of fixing with new deals and new business is not going to mend it?

So, what's to be done?

Do you bother to even go up the hill? What if like Jack and Jill going up the hill to fetch a pail of water, there is something at the top for you. Not climbing it isn't going to get it. Or is it?

Remember the story, or rather, the metaphor, of the animal. What happened when you tried to approach it and it wasn't ready to be approached? The animal turned and ran, and you after it, only to have lost it or caught it and been bitten. Or have a struggle ensue.

Now think back, yes I'll let you think just this once to when you let the animal approach you. You waited patiently enjoying the view and watching the animal and then when it was good and ready it took its steps to you, not the other way round. The end result, the animal let you pet it and even take it home.

No vinegar or brown paper in that story of truth, that's for sure.

Okay Julie-Ann that's all well and good when we're talking fluffy cute little bunnies in a field, and we have all the time in the world to hang around for them to approach us. That won't work in the cut-throat of business life when we have deadlines to meet and clients to find.

How do you know it won't work? Have you all been so busy doing it how you've always done it and missed the obvious?

Work isn't and doesn't have to be hard.

In fact work is so easy it is fun, timeless and you never have to run from it. Or to it. In fact, you never have to run again unless you really enjoy it. Then run as much as you like, but if you only run to get away from things or to try to get closer then here is my answer to that quandary. And it is a quandary, because how do you know when to approach and not to approach? How do you know when it is best to run for fun or run to try to catch something, or to escape from something you've just caught?

The answer couldn't be simpler.

You don't. And the reason you don't know is because

you've always done it that way. But what if you were to do it another way for a while and notice the difference? What if instead of approaching your clients, your boss, your workers you waited patiently and left it up to them to come to you?

What would happen?

Okay now stop thinking about what would happen, all the chaos and lack of money, respect, workers, work and eventually bankruptcy. And concentrate on letting the truth happen. You do know that what you think you get don't you? So your best bet if you can't think of anything positive is to stop thinking all together. After all, you have already created all that you really want in your life at some other time, but that's a different story to be told on another day when you're more up for it. For now we will stick with this one.

The Story Of The Woman And The Man

There once was a man who lived a very hectic life. He had children and his life focussed around them a lot of the time. Could he make enough money to pay maintenance and afford a nice place for them to be able to stay? Would he ever get the job he really wanted, or would he be destined to work for a corporation who did things, in his eyes, all backwards? They constantly fought about who was right, who could bring in the most money and quite frankly they had forgotten why they were in business in the first place. To offer opportunities to others to be able to grow and change by using the product or service that they were offering.

The woman, on the other hand, for there is nearly always another hand in your life, unless you decide to be as the woman. Free. The woman was free. Free to do as she did, to say as she said and to work when she chose, although work to her meant life and living and nothing else. Was she poor? No she was the richest person in the land. Why? How? How could this be? Well that you will find out later. For now, you just have to have some patience and let me tell you more about the man and the woman because these are intricate and important details for your mind to grab hold of and run with.

Do you still run?

Oh never mind, back to the story.

The man would get up tired and agitated and this would increase as the day went on, especially if it happened to be a designated workday. As it always was. Particularly as just lately he had changed jobs and was trying to make a name for himself in his new company. The day would drag, though there never, ever seemed to be enough hours in that day, or any other for that matter, to get everything done. Work would be taken home with him. Not only in the physical but the mental form as well.

And this was the man's problem, or at least one of them. You know he had the usual thing, aches and pains, skin complaints, lethargy, hyperactivity, and stress. All those things that everyone seems to be suffering from. Suffering who mentioned suffering? Not the woman that's for sure, she had long gone past the suffering stage she was more into the thoroughly enjoying and living and loving stage. But you'll find out more about the woman when we have finished with the man. For there is a lot to tell about the man. He led a very complicated life. The woman's was very simple and easy to follow.

The man ate all the wrong things and felt ill regularly. He drank and ate what he didn't like, to fit in with others doing the same. He said things he didn't mean to say or do things he didn't mean to do because he thought about them first. He didn't have much time for fun, or to see his kids. He was single and fairly happy being so but wanted the love of a good woman to make him complete. He didn't know this, but he acted that way. He would look for opportunities to grow and change at every step of the way instead of recognising he was and is the opportunity. He would be surprised and shocked when business started going his way, even when he knew, or thought he did, how good he was and what an asset he could become to his new company. He had forgotten to notice that he already was the asset and there was no becoming about it. He just was.

As was the woman. There is nothing much to tell of her. She enjoyed life. She worked for her living and lived for her work. The two were and are inseparable. Neither being hard or challenging, both being full of energy, love, and joy. As she was. She was also very kind, offering opportunities in abundance for others to grow and change and recognising the gifts she had to offer. She also readily received the gifts others liked to give her back for her services. Yet there were no services, just her. For she had found out who she was and now she was just doing what she knew best, being herself and nobody else. She never got ill and only ran when she wanted to and never for more than anything other than fun. She had everything she had ever dreamed of or desired and she shared this with others who had none. She never feared lack or bankruptcy or poverty for she knew as long as she is who she is this could and would never happen to her. And never is a long time. So, unlike the man, and this is the main difference that you will find. And really this difference only lies in your mind.

The only difference was the woman knew who she was and lived accordingly. The man was still searching and still believing in others rather than himself. He relied on others to bring him opportunities to change. The woman never ever changed. She remained constant like the wave. She had been the surfer, the board and the teacher and had reached the point of no return. She had reached her final destination and knew there was no more. This is how she was able to stop thinking about it and just do, be, say and live it. This is why the woman had lots of time for fun, work and pleasure, love, and money. For she knew that really she was all of those things. For giving opportunities to others brings abundance to you. The one who recognises and trusts in themselves and who they are. Not the one who has put all their trust in the way it has been done for years or in another's way.

The woman knew this well and that is why the woman trusts in no man, only herself.

The man trusts in everyone other than himself.

The woman has and always can and will have, all that she ever wants or could dream of. The man has nothing, or what he does have he has to work hard at for someone else to give it to him.

The woman simply receives gratefully. The man asks and doesn't feel worthy when he gets.

The woman loves herself and everyone else. The man has problems; issues that he needs to sort out before he could try to think about actually loving himself or even thinking about letting others love him for who he is. Then and only then, he might start to like everyone, but love? He could work on that if he could find the time. Time, that's a sore subject at the moment, but he could try. Try, yes, life was very trying. Life, what's that, as he spends most of his time at the office he didn't really have a life, well not of which you could speak. Speak, oh yes he did lots of that, and a lot of it unnecessary probably because of all the thinking he had to do before and after he had spoken to make sure he had said the right thing and didn't offend anyone or put his foot in his mouth, as he had been so used to doing for so many years. Ah yes, his past, now that was a nightmare and one that kept coming back when he least expected it to. Trust, how could he? Things don't just fall into your lap do they?

Or do they?

The woman didn't need to think and only spoke when she had something to say.

The woman knew that things do fall into your lap when you stop wanting and let go. Then you end up with what you wanted in the first place.

The woman had the key, letting go and acceptance and was always invited in through open doors.

The man kept getting closed doors, slammed in his face with regrets, refusals and lots of stress and pain.

The woman had none of this and only received more and more joy and love and happiness and all things that she had wished for.

Why?

Because the woman knew and believed in whom she was. The man still continued to search and distrusted what he found.

Until you can truly believe in yourself then you will always get what you've always got. When you let go and trust that what you want will just be handed to you on a plate, then and only then, does it come.

If you persist in chasing the animal it will just keep on running. If you hang around and waste your life waiting and waiting because you are so desperate for it to approach you then you will hang around waiting and waiting. A fool is always left wanting. Yet a wise man is wise enough when to wait and when to act.

Some animals will allow you to approach them slowly bit by bit until you are right next to them. They get more comfortable the nearer you come to them. Others just cannot stand you moving or even trying to get closer. So how do you know when to approach or not to approach?

Let's take this back to real life and forget animals and women and men and talk about clients. Because that's what the most important thing in business is, the clients, right?

Wrong.

The most important thing in business is not the client, not the business or the people in it, but you. Without you, your business would not exist. Yes the business may still exist, you are not indispensable for the business to go on, and no one is. The business would not be the same though without you, because nobody can replace who you are, you are unique.

And who are you?

If you really don't know the answer to this question then I suggest you find out because I personally would not like to conduct business with someone or a company that wasn't sure whether they were Martha or Arthur. Are you the woman or the man?

This isn't about gender. This is about trust and belief in you. This is about knowing when to approach and when not to approach. And the only way you can really know that is by knowing you. No one else knows what you feel inside or why you do what you do in the way that you do. That is completely unique to you. That is what makes you, you. So nobody can tell you what to do or when it's right to do something, not even your boss although they will try, after all it's their job to. But do they know who they are? Are you following orders from someone who is just as lost as yourself? Does the blind leading the blind help anybody get to the destination that you are all trying to get to? Do you even know what the destination is if neither you, your manager, or the company etc can see it? Or are you all so lost that you have forgotten the destination and gone off in lots of different directions to find the ending? Wouldn't life be easier and more productive and profitable for all concerned in your personal and professional life if you knew whom you were?

Then without question you would know exactly when to approach and when not to approach. Call it intuition or gut instinct or sixth sense, there would be something inside of you that will let you know the time is right now, and you will do exactly what you know you are meant to do, at the precise moment that sets all the wheels in motion and opens all the doors.

Until that time focus on really finding out about yourself and the company and other people you work for or with. Make sure that you are all of the same sex, when it comes to how you write your stories. If half of you act like the woman and half of you like the man then I suppose you've got a fifty-fifty chance of success. If however all of you are like the man in the story, then you have a sure-fire way of eventually getting what you want. But at what cost?

Divorce?

Lots of unnecessary hard work and research?

Health problems?

Stress?

Obesity or malnutrition?

Bankruptcy or redundancies?

Loss of friends and or colleagues?

Lost identity?

And more

If you are all like the woman in the story and know when the time is right to do what you have to do then you will only ever get reward upon reward for your patience and hard work. Did I say hard? I meant to say 'easy' because work would no longer be hard it would just flow and be so easy you will have to think of another word to call it, apart from work. Maybe you could call it life and then you will really understand what it means to live your work?

It's just a thought. Or rather it isn't a thought, it's just a fact.

So, approach if you want and if the time is wrong you had better have the bandages handy because you might end up getting your fingers bitten, or worse still lose the deal you were chasing.

The choice is yours. You always have choice. That is, if you are really being you. If you're not then the choice always falls into someone else's lap, oh, by the way, so do the rewards. Still if that's the ending you want to your story then go for it. I wish you all the luck because you're going to need it. If it isn't and you're partial to happy endings, a bit like me, then sit tight and listen to the voice inside that knows when it's right for you to approach and when it is definitely not right. That way not only do the deals fall into your lap but all the rewards and acclaims that go with it do too.

That's it on approaching or not, the rest is up to you.

7 WHO'S RIGHT, ME OR YOU?

How do you know that what I say or write isn't just a load of rubbish made up through my own ideas of grandeur or delusions?

You don't unless you have experienced it first-hand. This is the only way you can ever know that what someone says is true, by it being your truth. Not just theirs but yours. And there will be lots of times in your life when you come across weird and wonderful ideas, concepts, or new ways of being or doing things and they will go way over your head and level of understanding and that is fine and how it is meant to be. You cannot force yourself to change or understand anything or everything that you hear. It just wouldn't be fair on your tiny mind.

And our minds are tiny until we let them expand further and further out and beyond our normal range of thinking. Then and only then, will you find your own inner truth. Not by reading a book or listening to someone speak but by opening your mind to the point of no return and letting universal knowledge and wisdom enter into your head as it has done mine.

How do I know that what I write is true?

- Because I'm writing it

- I'm believing it

- I'm living it and have first- hand proof of everything I've written coming true.

How?

Because I went on a journey to find out who I was so once again I could help you. If you don't want my help then that is fine. If you do then I'm glad to be of service.

And that is what it boils down to. You and your company, corporation, business, job whatever you call it, are here to offer a service to another. Now, the service I offer is How To Be You, in words written and spoken in many different ways and formats for all to comprehend whether they are young or old, for personal or professional use. I do this to the best of my ability. The only way I can do this is to know what I have written and am offering is true by actually being the end result of my words. Therefore if you ever meet me and I hope you do, you will know that what I speak of is true.

So, what do you offer in way of a service to another? Are you clear about who you personally, professionally or as a company or corporation really are? Have you delved beneath the surface, taken off the many layers and masks other people have adorned you with and seen the truth? Are you really who you first thought or is there really more to you than meets the eye?

Are you living and being your truth or is there some discrepancy in the service you offer and who you say you are?

If the shoe were on the other foot and you were your own client would you know exactly what service you were getting or what to expect from you? And would you as the client be happy with the explanation as to why you were offering this service in the way you do? Are your methods out-dated and you as a person or company have changed yet you have failed to recognise this as the truth and catch up with yourself? Do you and your colleagues work in the best way possible or is there room for change? Are you waiting for the animal that left a long time ago? Or do you know exactly when is the right time to approach or not? Have you become so far away from your original thoughts and ideas on which you had belief either personally, professionally or as a whole that you have denied the truth that lies right in front of you?

And what if you have? What if, as a person, or a company/corporation you have outgrown yourself and not fully recognised to the extent of whom you have become? What do you do then?

Do you run and hide and try to bury what you have just realised?

Do you start the messy job of uncovering all the layers around you to find out the truth of you, individually or as a whole? Believe me it is a messy job. If you don't believe me then read 3 of my previous books, *How To Be You, A Story With A Difference, Life, Death And The Universe,* and *Fact*

Or Fiction? You Decide, and you'll soon know what I'm talking about.

Do you get someone else to take your pain away and tell you who he or she thinks you are?

Or do you do something else instead?

And if you choose to do something else instead what could that be?

Would you continue to read books like this one or different, searching for the answers to your problems?

Would you ask another for their advice, or even borrow their identity? I'm sure at least one of you has done that before now, I know I have, and it's not a pleasant site. Dressing up how another wants you to. Marrying or dating the person that somebody thinks you should. Working for the company that you think is right but know is wrong for you. Marketing the wrong product or in the wrong way because that's how it's always been done. And so on and on and generally just not being yourself at all.

Or would you do as I have done, and this is only a suggestion, and throw the books away and sit and listen to yourself. Only you know the answer and the right way forwards for you. I can't tell you and nobody else can. We can guide you but at the end of the day it's your call. Do you call out your own name for help or do you keep running hoping you'll bump into the right person along the way?

I chose to run. I could have run for England except I wasn't in England because I'd ran to America to escape myself. Trouble was I followed myself. In fact I seemed to turn up wherever I went. And this is how it is, if you don't turn and face the truth sooner or later it will come up to you and hit right between the eyes. And when it does you sure do know it. I've had that happen on more than one occasion and on every time it has been a new revelation and opened my mind just a little bit more. It has almost felt as if I have been slowly walking up a flight of stairs until I reached the top and then it seems like I'm walking back down again. And in a way I am. For now I know what I know, and I've climbed the ladder of understanding I can come back down and teach what I know to others who are stuck on the first rung.

This is in no way condescending this is just how it is. For me anyway, and as long as you look outside of yourself for reasons, thoughts, and answers then that is how it will remain for you until the day you change it. Maybe that day is today or maybe not?

So if not, then let's take a closer look at this ladder of understanding.

The Ladder Of Understanding

The ladder of understanding has many layers or rungs, as I like to call them. Somehow it makes them easier to grab hold of. Each rung is slightly higher up and more expansive than the next until you get to the top where there are no more limitations to your thinking. But that's a long way off yet. So let me guide you rung by rung to where you want to go.

I'm assuming you want to get to the top. That's where most professionals want to go. You don't, you're different? Well good for you, then maybe you can learn this and become the leader or guide of the other ones and be the first to throw this book away?

The first rung is the very easy and basic one. You don't have a clue what anyone is saying, and you don't really care. You are content just being looked after and all your needs being met when you want them. (Sounds like the top one to me!) So this is rather like when you are a baby. You need shelter, love and food and you get it before you even know you need it. (Definitely sounds like the top rung to me.) And you don't even lift a finger to get it. (Yep, it is the top rung, how uncanny is that? The first rung is also the top one, interesting!)

The second rung is a little bit more advanced than the bottom one, although a lot less advanced than the top one. (Sound strange? All will be revealed as you continue to climb.) Bear with me as you have to walk at your pace I'm not going to carry you. And on this rung you are carried. You start to notice there is more to life than food, love, and shelter and that if you demand, then you can have it. So this is the demanding level, for you and definitely for anyone around you.

Next comes the third rung. This is an interesting rung as it has two sides to it. Or rather two ways of climbing it. You can choose to climb it on your own two feet, or by someone else's. This level of understanding comes from 'suck it and see' mentality. Try it once and if it works then okay, I'll do it again. Or try it once and if it doesn't work then I'll either do it again because a) I like pain, b) I'm a slow learner or c) I'm downright stubborn and hate change. So this level comes with a lot of internal and external conflict. Shall I, shan't I? You know the sort of thing.

Probably you know it as those overactive conversations you have in your head every morning when you decide what tie to wear or shoes to put on, which brief case to take or whether to drive or walk, run, or take a taxi. You get the picture. Oh yeah, this level or rung should I say, I've never been one to follow the natural, or thought the natural, way of doing things. This rung also encourages you to start to visualise and learn how to create your own reality by imagining how you want your future to be. All well and good if you want to stay on this rung for the rest of your life. And some people do. That's fine if you understand that your mind creating what you want, also creates what you don't want, like the pain and the challenges that go with this lack of understanding and respect for yourself. For there isn't a lot of respect going on at this rung. In fact there is quite a lot of fighting. Apart from the internal and external fights we've already talked about, there is another even bigger one. And that is the you who is already on the next level and rung fighting with the you that is down here stuck and refusing to go anywhere for fear of not getting everything they have imagined and dreamed of.

Now you've got a problem.

If you're not careful this rung could keep you there for a very long-time reliving pain and the past and fighting with yourself and others until you eventually fall off and end up back on rung one, and not in a good way. Usually you hurt yourself badly and when you are a child it is okay to be at rung one and dependent on everyone for all your needs but as an adult it isn't. Again I've been there, and it isn't a happy place.

So, what do you do?

Every step of the way up or down you accept just where you are today, get used to that place and then move on up when you are ready. Eventually you get to the top rung and then you can look back down on exactly where you have come from. For now appreciate you are moving up the ladder and I will see you up the top.

Each new rung after the last opens your mind and increases your self-awareness more and more until you really do understand who you are. Each new step brings new opportunities to grow and change until you realise there is no more need for growth and change and you are ready to remain constant within and bring the opportunities to others around you. And each new step brings its own rewards for your new labour. Until you recognise that no labour is involved, and you have reached the top of your ladder.

That's when life gets really easy. As long as you remember these things:

- Don't ever try to carry anyone up your ladder, they have to make it up in their own way and at their own pace.

- Never look down at anyone or be unkind when you reach the top as you only end up hurting yourself when you fall off, which you will.

- Always accept who you are whichever rung you happen to be on and don't let others telling you who they think you are make you doubt your position in life.

That's it. Stick to those three rules and climbing ladders will soon become your hobby. And with all the free time you will have left over you will definitely now have time to do some more things that you enjoy apart from work. And if you haven't, well then don't worry, there's always another rung for you to climb. In fact you can put as many rungs as you want to your ladder, or you could try one like mine and just have three and then the end result. It's entirely up to you how many you choose. And nobody can tell you otherwise unless you choose to listen to them.

What makes a good Chief Executive Officer

Their drive? Their motivation? Their ability to get things done? Their need for perfection or more? Their honesty and trust in their selves and their abilities?

Their trust in the people they employ to manage the company? Or maybe just the fact that they strive to get to where they are and once there they acknowledge their position and accept their role knowing they deserve it?

It doesn't matter where you are in the corporate ladder or your own personal understanding ladder. What is important that at the top, middle or bottom you know exactly where you are, whom you are and what you are going to do now you have reached this far. It's no good working hard all of your life to make promotion or get to the top of the tree only to find that when you are there you don't know what to do. Or worse still don't and can't accept that you have actually made it.

Ladders and trees they are all the same. CEO's and mail people, they are all the same. After all, ladders and trees are both made out of wood and CEO's and mail people are all made out of flesh and bones. No one is ever better or worse than you. There should be no rivalry as you climb your way upwards. Friendship and camaraderie can take you higher than judgement and jealousy. Pride comes before a fall. That is not to say you can't be proud of yourself, you can. Especially if you have been so hard on yourself that's how you got to where you are today. Then you need all the love and kindness you can find. If you don't start giving to yourself first then you will not get it back and will not have enough to share.

Nobody likes somebody who doesn't like him or herself. It's a well-known fact that if you are cruel to another then really you are being cruel to yourself. The difference is you are using someone else's name rather than your own. The wound ends up in the same place who's ever name you choose to use, and it's always in you.

And what's in a name anyway? Who says I am right, and you are wrong? Just because I am writing this book doesn't mean a thing. Just because I have one name and you have another doesn't mean anything. Names are just words placed on objects, people, and positions to satisfy our inquisitive mind.

If you were to wake up tomorrow and somebody told you that you were actually at the top of your company and could go no further and they had a name for it of Chief Executive Officer, what would you do?

I know I would probably panic and ask how it could be true. Then when the fear had subsided I would look at my history and realise why I had made it to the top of the ladder. And actually if the truth be told, I have been there for a long time, I just didn't realise it. And if you don't realise it then how can you accept it or you? You can't. So take away the name and what are you left with? You, that's who, and who are you? Oh that old question again.

Don't you know yet or have you begun to work it out? Have you sat down and looked through all the evidence of what you have in front of you and how you got here today? Or do you just trust and know that you are where you are and the more you accept that the more you will understand what you are supposed to do now you are here. And that goes for your business as well. If you can't accept who you are, then how can you possibly accept who or what you are working for or have become a part of? You can't.

Acceptance starts at home and then moves on from there, the same as everything else. It all starts at home and as home is where your heart is then that's where you should be looking. Not in the pages of someone else's book for your answer as to who is right, you or me? You should be ready to look inside of you. That is the only way to the real answer for you. And if you don't feel quite ready then maybe your coffee pot is still half full?

8 THE COFFEE POT OF TIME

Has she really gone mad, talking about coffee pots or is there some hidden meaning to it?

Yes, to both of those questions. But we won't worry about both of them for now let's just look at my madness. No, only joking. You've got to be able to have a laugh about yourself and life otherwise you would go mad. Especially when you find out who you are now, that's when heads will start to turn and the biggest turn of all will be yours. I'll leave you to experience that pleasure when it happens. For now let's talk coffee pots. I myself haven't drunk coffee for years, but that doesn't matter because this is just another metaphor to help unwind and open your mind to a new way of thinking. And that's all the coffee pot is. Well, that and just a little bit more.

Let me explain.

First I would like to dedicate this chapter to a good friend of mine that allowed me to give him the opportunity to change, which in turn changed me. And for that I am grateful.

Imagine that you have a large coffee pot that is in your head. This coffee pot is always percolating new coffee granules to make fresh coffee for you to drink, a bit like the one in your office or staff resting room. Just suppose, for a moment, that the coffee granules represented new information or ways of thinking and being. This information enters your head, the coffee pot, and takes its time percolating and slowly dripping drop by drop down through the machine changing from solid form to liquid, a more flowing palatable substance. The information from another or even you goes in hard and comes out soft and pleasing to the taste. Now as the granules are being percolated so the coffee drink can be formed, so too is the information you have gathered. We, as people, have many layers of understanding, the ladder is merely one way of looking at it there are hundreds and thousands of ways of learning and knowing how your mind works. Again the coffee pot is just another way. As this information drips down it goes through each level or layer of understanding until it becomes so much a part of you, you have embodied it as your truth. Rather like when the coffee is ready you drink it, and it becomes part of you.

And that is exactly how it is with new ways and new information, in the head and into the coffee pot of time. The mind mulls it over and chews on lots of different thoughts that stem from it. The coffee pot percolates. The mind allows the information to drip down slowly through various layers of understanding including:

- I don't agree, and this is complete rubbish.

- There could be some truth in that, and I would like to wait and see what happens next.

- Not sure but it would be amazing if it were true.

- No way could I believe anything other than that, but how is it possible?

Again these are just a few layers that the information and coffee filters down through until you reach the final one.

- Without a doubt that is right.

Now the coffee is ready to drink. Now you have embodied the truth and now you can live it. Simple as that.

The coffee pot takes time to percolate the granules and so does your mind. There is no need for frustration or over activity of the mind to speed up the process. It won't. You have to wait and let it happen naturally. Only you know how many layers and old beliefs your new wisdom has to get through before it can truly hit you between the eyes. And when it does then you really do know, and then you will understand what I mean when the truth hits you. That is what it feels like. It's as if somebody comes and smacks the truth down right in front of you so you can see what it is that you have been missing for so long. Although when the truth reaches, you know it wasn't missing at all, you just thought it was.

So, even if you don't drink coffee, then who cares. What you should be caring about is what level of understanding is the new information that you have read or heard laying at and how much further has it to go until it does hit you. And if you don't care about it then maybe the truth has already been told and you are just on the verge of receiving it. The more you care and worry about it the more you will block it. If when the percolator is doing what percolators do, you kept on checking inside it eventually you would stop it from doing its job. And that's what it is like with your mind. And maybe you have found this with your work or your clients. The more you persist the more they resist. Just like the animal that runs from you, so too will the truth if you chase it. If however you stand still and let it come to you through all the layers of your present understanding then it will come a lot quicker. And you will be able to enjoy the results of your patience. A nice hot cup of steaming coffee or in my case, a cool glass of water. Or in your case, and everyone else who has applied this analogy to their mind, abundance, abundance, and more abundance. And abundance comes in whatever way you choose it to:

New jobs

New clients

More money

More time

More understanding

Whatever way you want abundance to appear it will. For you are the real creators of your life no one else. And as soon as you start to recognise this then you can get on creating the life you want without having to even leave your own home, or wherever you may be staying at when the coffee becomes ready for the drinking. How wonderful would that be?

To be able to have all that you want, when you want it and really have to do very little other than recognise who you are, why you are here and what to do about it now you know?

Well, stick with me kids and you can. Or rather don't stick with me or anyone else and branch out on your own in whatever way that means to you and make a dent in the market of what you know you are offering. Cause a stir with people who know you and show them what you and your company or business really are made of. Be you through and through, whoever you decide you are and remain true to that identity

forever more. Consistency is nine tenths of the law; the other tenth is not jumping from who you are to who you think you are. Same thing? Yes it is. And so is all of what I have been saying to you over and over. I have just been saying it to you in different ways to chip away at your various levels of knowledge and understanding so that you may reach the top of your ladder with less pain and irritation than you may well have originally.

So if I can ever be of service to any of you then please don't hesitate to call me. My name is Julie-Ann, life guru, the wave, writer, fortune teller, business coach, life coach, spiritual healer, master practitioner of neuro linguistic programming, inspirational speaker, hypnotherapist, aromatherapist and masseur, nurse, the woman in the story, the man in the story, the wise man and the fool, the leader, the pioneer, the CEO of my world and many more 'labels.'

But what's in a name or a qualification it doesn't really tell you who you are. Or does it? Does your name or your abilities really give you clues? Do we naturally gravitate to what we are good at and enjoy through our life or do we just follow the image of someone else's opinions and needs for us?

Are you in your job for you or for another?

Do you enjoy what you do, or do you suffer in what you do?

Are you doing what you do for yourself, being yourself or are you being someone else to please someone else?

Does your place of work or your business/company/corporation do what it wants to do, or has it fallen into the trap of only providing what the client wants and not what the company really is here to offer?

How can a client know what he/she/they want if you haven't given them an option as to what is available? Maybe you or your company have exactly what has been missing from their life only they don't know it because you don't know it. That is why it is so important to know whom you are, why you are here and what you do now you know that. Answer those three questions and life will never be the same for you again.

What happens if, try as you might, you just can't answer them? Or you know roughly who you or your company is and why you think you are here, but how can you be sure that you are right?

Because my friends when that truth hits you right between the eyes there is no mistaking that feeling for anything else in the world. That is when there is absolutely no doubt in your mind that the coffee has well and truly percolated and is ready for tasting. And that is when all hell lets lose. Only it is as far from hell as you could imagine. Heaven would be a better way of describing it, although that's just another word to satisfy your curious mind.

If you want to know what it's really like then you are just going to have to wait and see for yourself aren't you?

And if you can't?

Well, if you can't then you may as well start dressing like a man because that's who you are in the story of your life.

Remember a watched pot never boils and a coffee percolator takes as long as it wants to take to produce a great cup of coffee, not how long you are encouraging it to. Leave it alone and then enjoy the rewards. Touch it now and you could ruin the flavour forever.

In other words do what you are doing and let whatever is about to happen, happen because the sheer fact that you are reading this book means you have already started to climb up your ladder of understanding and who knows maybe you're already at the top you just don't realise how far you are yet. But you will. Leave the pot to time and you will find out exactly who you or your company/business/corporation or work is and why you are here and then you will be able to get on and do exactly what you are here to do. And that is definitely with as much fun, enjoyment, health, wealth, and whatever other good things you can manage to create. Just stop managing them and they will fall into your lap one by one, drip, drip, drip and create the best cup of coffee yet.

May I suggest that you go away and spend time letting the coffee settle, for the next part will blow your mind and burst the percolator in to tiny little pieces.

9 WHEN PAST BECOMES FUTURE AND BEYOND

This may take you some time to get used to and when you have, this will definitely not only change you as a person but also the whole way you do business or run your company.

Just suppose, for one moment, that the man and the woman in the previous story are really the same person. One is the present you and one is the future you. Okay, so far that's easy enough to comprehend. That means the woman is how you want to be in the future and the man is how you are now being, all stressed out and distrusting of yourself.

Right, let's take it a step further. The man is only being like he is because he hasn't realised that the future has already happened. Whereas the woman has realised and can then trust completely in what she does in the present to walk into her future. The man thinks he has to create the future from his past and present. The woman knows that she has already been out and created the perfect future for herself and all she now has to do is live it in the physical way today.

The man thinks this is total madness and sets up an internal conflict with the woman who is really the man's future self. Hence an argument begins, and faults happen in the present which delay and change the future that was already there waiting for you.

If this is way over your head then don't worry, just understand it at a comfortable level for you and eventually one day, when you are ready and the coffee has dripped through, you will understand it as it is written. For now, it is enough to be aware that you are living two lives. One here and now, in your present, and the other in the future, creating a world and life of abundance. That is how you know when to approach and when not to approach because in some other time you already have and had the results.

To make this easier let me tell you a story:

The Chief Executive Officer And The Maid

Once upon a time there lived a Chief Executive Officer (known as a CEO from now on) and his maid. They lived in the CEO's house happily together for a number of years. The CEO was a nice enough guy and was fairly easy to get on with. Although he did have one trait, he liked things done exactly his way, regardless of whether anyone knew better. The maid was used to this and quietly went off and did things her way, which she knew that was best. The CEO never knew about this until today.

Today was like any ordinary day. The CEO got up, had breakfast, took a morning stroll, and came in to do some work on his computer. He wasn't going into the office today, as there was no need. He trusted in the managers he had appointed, and he was happy letting them get on with their jobs. Leaving him to get on with his. After all what was the point of being at this level of the ladder if you couldn't trust in others to do the jobs for you and enjoy being here? There was none. So he knew he had plenty of spare time today to do things he liked.

The maid knew this also and she had known it for a long time as she had seen and helped the CEO get to where he was without him knowing this. Of course she couldn't ever tell him because he hadn't been ready to hear, until today that is.

The day started off as any ordinary day for the maid. She got up, stretched, did her chores, and then went on a journey. It was only a short journey as she had done most of her work a while back so she too was coming to the point where she could rest and enjoy being at the top of her ladder. Her journey, though short, took her half way across the world and back. She had to see a man about a dog, as we English like to say. She had to sort out some appointments in some far-off lands for the CEO. The maid did all of this and was still back in time to fix the CEO's breakfast.

How did she do that?

Because the maid knew how to travel in time. In fact, she didn't just know it, she was it. The maid was the future of the CEO. He didn't know it until today and now he is finding out it is coming as a bit of a shock to him. But given time he will get used to it and understand what benefits this has for him in the way he lives today.

Imagine a world that you have already created in the future. Imagine that whilst you are out sleeping, the maid in you, who works only for you, goes out and creates the life that you will be living tomorrow, today. She knows what you in the present have been striving for and want and she goes and gets it.

When you wake up all you have to do is go with those gut instincts of whether something is right or not and walk straight into it. All you have to do is live each moment today with ease and joy knowing that tomorrow has well and truly been taken care of. All you have to do is listen to your wise inner voice, the maid in you that you may once have thought as the wise man and do what you know is right for you. Say what you know you need to say today. See what you know you need to see today.

When you know your future has been taken care of, then all you have left to do is live in the present moment.

And it is only a moment. Everything could change in the next moment, and it already has. You have already seen to that.

When the CEO, that you are, and the maid, that you are, stop being in conflict then everything runs smoothly in your personal and professional life. You never get ill, miss out on a deal or a chance to offer another person an opportunity to grow and change. You never need for anything and always get what you want. As long as it is what you want. Sometimes you can think it is what you want because you feel some resistance and life in the past has told you this is a good sign. Well, sorry to disagree but I'm here to tell you otherwise. If you have resistance to anything, be it something simple that you want to eat or drink, or something you want to say, or a business deal you want to conduct, then listen to that resistance and know it is the maid in you telling you that is not the right path to go down.

For that is what it is. We are merely walking two paths of life. One is our future that the maid in us has already gone out and created and fine adjusted to suit our desires and needs. The other is the present that our minds and our bodies like to be stimulated by today.

We are all time travellers. We just don't know it, until today. Now you do.

This is not fantasy made up from a bored mind. This is reality. I only speak my truth and I only live my truth. All of my books have been written about my future either minutes, hours, or days before they actually happen to me in the present. Everything I have written here has happened to me as I write it or is about to happen. That is how, and the only way, I know what I write is true. I am the maid, which writes these books, and I am the CEO that lives them in the present.

How is this so?

Because we are merely energy trapped inside a physical body with a physical mind that likes to think and think and think. We do not use our minds enough for what they are here for. We use them only on a destructive level, or so we think. Actually we are using our higher minds to go out and create the future and change the past if it needs changing. We are able to create the future that we want in the best way possible, trying out all the different scenarios so that when we eventually catch up with ourselves and we walk into our future, all we get is abundance and ease, instead of the usual expected pain, torment, irritation, blocks, and barriers to our success. These only come from our logical mind creating our future in the present.

If you know that your future has been created once in the very best, most rewarding way for you, why on earth would you want to try to interfere and create it again using the CEO of today?

You wouldn't unless you didn't trust the maid. Then why employ her in the first place if you didn't trust her? Why not sack her now and be done with it and carry on creating more pain and confusion and believing in the chaos theory because you are the chaos? Why forget that you live on earth and that means you have this power? The power of the mind to create beauty, love, health, wealth, and happiness around and for you, without doing anything other than believing in your employees. After all you are the fool and the wise man. The fools, if you continue to do the work that you have paid someone else to do. And the wise men, if you give up the ghost and let the maid get on with her job.

Let lady love shine in you. Bring lady luck into your life, work, business, company, clients whatever or whoever enters into your life will always have the opportunity to learn from the way you do things, until they learn from the way they do things. This is the difference between the fool and the wise man, the man and the lady, the CEO, and the maid. One knows and trusts and just does, the other cogitates, debates, encourages, stops, prevents, orders, worries and generally makes a mess of things by doing it alone or by another's advice. Sometimes they get to the top, but we have already mentioned the cost of that journey. And what if when you're up the top you realise you've really climbed up someone else's ladder and not your own?

Then what?

Do you stay there and make do? Is that what you are doing today?

Or do you climb back down, learn from your mistakes, and start the ascent up your own ladder this time with wisdom and purpose?

Only when you trust yourself do you not only make it to CEO level, but you remain there happy and grateful to yourself for creating this opportunity for you to expand. To expand your mind to the point of no return. To expand your mind where your coffee pot and time no longer exist and to expand your mind to the point where you no longer exist.

Well not as you used to anyway.

Although, if you take a look back over your life and the chapters of this book then you will actually realise that you have always existed in this way, you just didn't know it. Until now. And now you do, now what?

Nothing.

Nothing. I can't just do nothing! How will anything get done if I do nothing?

Because everything has been done. You, my friends, just have to walk into it and enjoy the pleasures of being on this earth in this body with this incredible mind and knowing that there are more of you like it. And now you know this, you will start attracting more people who understand and accept you and the way you do business. Because that is what you have just created for yourself by reading this chapter. No more struggle, pain, or strife, just one big happy, fulfilled life.

Now, take that to a deeper level and use your new knowledge and way of thinking in your work and business. Think about how much money and time, effort, workers, and pain you will save if you were to adopt this new way of being. And really there isn't a new way to it or you at all, it's merely the way you look at it. If you have always looked on the darker side of life then that is what you have ended up with because your day has been created by the mind of tomorrow. If, however, you have been able to look on the brighter side of life then that is what you have and will continue to get, for the day now has been created by the mind of tomorrow. Yes, both minds of tomorrow have created the future for you but which one created yours, bright or dark?

Have you got a dark, troubled future just waiting for you to walk or crawl into because that is the way your mind thinks? Or have you got a nice bright, light, and abundant future waiting for you to ease yourself into?

I know what mine is. But mine isn't important and isn't the one in question, yours is?

Don't worry if your future looks bleak because you can always change your mind. How do you do that?

Read on and find out.

10 CHANGING YOUR MIND FOR THE BETTER

If you have had years of thinking in one particular way, how can you just suddenly change your mind for the better? And how can you even start to believe that it could be for the better and that it isn't a load of rubbish and a ploy to get you to read more books?

That's an interesting question and one that I would like to answer with openness and complete honesty. And because I never do anything that I don't want to, then I will answer this question in the way I want to, with complete openness and honesty.

Do you ever catch yourself doing something that you don't want to do?

Come on, there must be at least one time in your life when you have given in and done something that you know wasn't right for you to do but you somehow managed to let yourself or someone else talk you into it?

I know I have. And I would be lying if I didn't tell you I've done it more times than I can remember and even very recently. Particularly when it came to business or relationships. That was always my downfall, until now.

This morning I learnt what I am writing here to you today on October 1st, 2004. I learnt that I am and have been a time traveller all my life as so have and are all of you reading this. The one thing that stops us from understanding it is the very thing that helps us to do it, our minds. Without our minds we would not be here today. And without our minds I would not be writing this about tomorrow that I am just about to write. For tomorrow does always come. It comes in the form of today. Tomorrow is merely a word for the future that you have already lived in one dimension and have brought back the knowledge for you in the here and now today.

I know that tomorrow at 11 am there will be a slight earthquake in San Francisco measuring 3.2 on the Richter scale and nobody will get hurt. I know this to be true as I was there watching it happen. It happened on the San Andreas Fault just about in the middle due north of it. There will be more and more, and we need to stop them. The only way we can do this is to change our way of thinking and realise that we are creating them in this present life by our thoughts about tomorrow.

Our thoughts are very powerful and do in fact create our world of tomorrow.

What if I'm right and there is an earthquake tomorrow?

Did I create it or was it going to naturally happen? Well we will never know unless we start to change our way of thinking and let our future change with it. So many people think bad thoughts that this interferes with the good future that awaits you and your business or company and creates a troubled future for all concerned. Trouble breeds more trouble and problem after problem to sort it out and get the equilibrium back.

Whether you really believe in what I am saying or not is of no consequence to me, or you. But it will be to your life and your business. If you don't at least explore the possibility that you are your own creator and that you are creating the future that you will live today, tomorrow. Then you will always end up with a mediocre future life and business. You will continue to work hard for very little rewards and never have enough or be enough whatever you do, be it personally or professionally. If however, you allow yourself to open your mind then this is how you change your mind for the better. The more open your mind becomes; the more possibilities of living enter into it and eventually into your present day. The past catches up with the present and you realise that you have been creating your future all along.

Now really think about what that does mean to you and the world as a whole? If you fully understand that you create your own future in the only way possible that causes complete and utter abundance and delight for you, at every step of the way. As long as you trust the maid and let her get on with her job of doing this then you as the CEO can go on permanent retirement when it comes to worrying and thinking or planning. When you accept you've already created it for you, or your company, then that is the time you really do let go of the present control and ride on the back of you, the future, the wave into your next wonderful moment.

Take each moment at a time and know that the next will be just as good as, if not better, than the first. Notice over the next few days, if you have chosen to drink the coffee, how life just gets better and better for you. And it will continue to do this as long as you accept who you are, why you are here and what you should do about it now you know.

I am here to enjoy life. I am life and all that life is. And all I do about it is nothing because I know I've already done all I need to do to create the future life I want. In fact I've already seen it and have been seeing it for the past few years. I just didn't realise that is what I was doing. I thought I had an over active imagination now I know differently.

Do you?

Do you see yourself in the future, maybe in dreams or fleeting moments? Do you think that what you have seen or visualised is just your imagination? Or are you more open to it being something else? Are you more open to the fact that it is your future? Have you really changed your mind for the better?

The answer to that lies in your future doesn't it?

So, for now, I leave you with this thought:

If you are the man, the woman and the CEO and the maid

then who is really in control of your future me or you?

Confused? You will be if you try to rationalise or reason with it. Just put it as granules into your percolator and let it come out as sweet tasting coffee when you are ready for the next step, opening your eyes to the truth.

11 OPENING YOUR EYES TO THE TRUTH

Right, now is the time to finish the story of the CEO and the maid

You thought I had?

Well, I did tell you to stop thinking in the way you have been used to and open your mind and let new possibilities enter. Now you know why. Sometimes you may catch yourself doing something or saying something and you aren't rationally sure why. The rest of this story will explain:

The maid decided that today was a good enough day as any to sit the CEO down for a talk regarding his past, present and future. Or rather regarding her past, present, and future. Or actually the talk was about their future as a whole. Because she knew that was what needed to happen for the future to be rosy and just as the CEO wanted.

Before I go any further the CEO would just like to say a few words:

"Thank you. I'm sure that I don't need to say this, but I will anyway. (*He did a lot of that, talking unnecessarily.*) I would just like to clarify why the story relates to a CEO as a man and the maid as a woman, so there is absolutely no misunderstanding on your part. I do not come here to offend, degrade, classify, or act in any way sexist towards one character or the other. These names and genders are just that, names, and random genders. Given to the characters to explain the story and will become clearer as to why they were chosen as you read on. I also want to make it clear and apologise (*another thing that he always seemed to be doing, again unnecessarily*) that I only use the words Chief Executive Officer to describe somebody who has got to the top of their ladder. Whatever position you see yourself at is right for you. And remember we are all at the top of our ladders if not in the form of CEO then in the form of a maid. That's it from me, now I'll hand you back to the story."

So as you can see the CEO really did go out of his way to apologise and please others and this is why it had taken him so many years to reach the top of his ladder and with such hardship. He hadn't let the maid do it for him. He had taken over and decided that what he knew was best, or so he thought. The maid, and you, know different. And now the CEO was just about to find out the truth.

The maid asked the CEO to sit down as the truth may shock him somewhat. It definitely wouldn't hurt him. Only he could do that. The maid couldn't ever hurt him or another she just wasn't paid to do that. And as she only did what she was paid to do she never did hurt anyone especially not her master.

And who was her master? Who actually did pay her? You're about to find out.

The CEO took a seat and looked straight at the maid, he wanted to not only hear but also see everything that she said. He liked seeing things, unfortunately he had spent most of his life seeing what he thought was the truth and what he wanted to be the truth, as opposed to what actually was the truth. The maid knew this and that is why it was time for a talk. If the CEO kept on making up stories in his head then he was bound to face rack and ruin. Yet if he listened to what the maid had to say and finally see the truth for what it was, then he was all set for a blissful and abundant future.

The maid began and the CEO listened. The maid and the CEO talked for hours, or rather the maid talked and for once the CEO was speechless. He really didn't know what to say. Everything the maid said, even though a little or a lot off the wall, made perfect sense to him. He knew he had truly found a diamond in the maid that sat before him. Who was she? Where had she come from? Why had she chosen to work for him? He didn't know the answer to these questions himself so he knew what he must do. He must listen to the maid.

So the maid continued talking. She spoke in a language he had never understood before, but he did tonight, for day led into night. She spoke of such things and ways of being that he had only dreamed of and didn't really believe them to be true. She spoke of time travel and pleasure and the future and the past and all amazing things that you have heard of but dismiss for fear of them coming true to you. She spoke of knowledge from far off lands and future events that had not happened, not in his eyes anyway. And through all of this she spoke with the highest pleasure she could offer. She spoke with love in her tongue, her mouth, and her words. She spoke of the love that was open to him if he wanted it and the joy that this could bring. She spoke of the love he already had in his life today if he only opened his eyes a little wider and saw the truth staring back at him. She spoke of friendships and unions that he could never imagine would come true.

She spoke of so much the CEO thought his head would explode.

And that is eventually what happened. For the future and the past and the present to flow, the maid and the CEO have to become one. No longer is there an employee or employer, just two people who have joined together in harmony to bring whatever it is they want into their life today and tomorrow.

Before the CEO agreed to this, he knew it was the right thing to do. He knew that if he continued to filter all that he heard he would waste valuable time learning what he already knew. For before the CEO had made it that high up he too had been a maid. A maid to another. He had just forgotten this role and completely erased it from his memory. But this is how he knew what the maid said was true. He knew the truth hit you between the eyes and here it was now on this very day, at this very moment staring him right in the face. He knew that he could do no more and he had to leave the ghost of the past behind. For that is all he was, a ghost of his own mind. A memory of whom he had been, today. But he wasn't for he was and is and always was the maid. He just thought he wasn't. The CEO never climbed up or down anyone else's ladder or his own. He had always been there. At the top, looking down. The CEO had never, ever employed a maid to create his future or help live his past or present, he was the maid and always had been. Thought and reason had stopped him accepting this.

And now he knew he realised he really could not continue with this charade, this falsehood and lack of truth. He knew there was only one thing to do. He let his ghost die and any ideas of not being who he was.

And who was and is that? Who is the CEO/Maid? Do you know?

Have you opened your eyes to the truth about you? Or are they still tightly shut? If closed then maybe you can just take a peek at the next chapter and then the next and the next until you get to the end of this book and you finally realise who you are? Maybe, maybe not? Up to you.

Eyes open or closed?

If you keep them closed then unless you know how to see with the third eye in the middle of your forehead then may I suggest the rest of what I write will seem pretty dark to you as you won't be able to see it.

If you keep them open then maybe by the end of this book you will be ready for the next and the next that uncovers more about who I am and why I am here and what I am supposed to do now I know I'm no longer a CEO/Maid, but one.

Now look at the eyes of your work, your company, your business, or corporation. Are their eyes fully open and wide-awake to all the possibilities of life? Or are they still in two minds, split down the middle as to their role, purpose, service and reason for being here?

Do you as a person walk through life looking around at all there is to see? Or do you run with your head deep into the ground for fear of bumping into the truth?

Too late. You just have. Here I am and I'm right in front of you.

What are you going to do now?

Hide some more behind that mask you keep making for yourself? Or come out fighting and accept what you know and no more?

Or would you rather practice opening those beautiful eyes just a little wider and wider until one day you wake up and you no longer need to read the truth because you are the truth? One day will you arise and find that you have gone off the coffee, as there is no longer a need for a percolator in your mind anymore?

Until that time let me share a cup of coffee with you, for the last time, as the maid and the CEO. And you decide which you are and then you have your answer to the previous question left unanswered, is it me creating your future or you?

12 LIFE, BUT NOT AS YOU KNOW IT

I'm presuming the maid and the CEO no longer exist and that story is long dead in the water as you now recognise that you are the wave and not the surfer, board, or teacher. So now what?

What happens next?

Do you go off and live life like you always have done by? A little by chance and a lot by interference of your conscious mind.

Or do you just let whatever will be unfold in front of you not really knowing how, but always aware that it will and in the most wonderful way that is right for you?

Do you conduct your business as you have always done?

Or do you learn from what you have read, and I have written and start to understand who you really are and why you are here as an individual and as a whole?

Do you let yourself be open to more truth?

Or do you close your eyes now before any more can come to you?

Are you to remain scared of the possibilities that life and you have to offer yourself and your business?

Or do you open your arms and graciously greet each one and enjoy this new way of living and thinking?

Do you let go of all thoughts as you know them and let your higher mind think for you?

Or do you continue to think on the low level and create only what you know, or think is true?

Do you let all that is yours come to you now in abundance and with no conscious interfering?

Or do you persist in forging your way as you think, or have been told you should?

Are you really ready to live and work a life that has not been told?

Or do you wish to repeat my stories over and over?

Are you the maid or the CEO?

Or are you the whole and the truth of the matter in hand?

Your hands, no one else's. You do not need another to create your life or your reality if you accept that you have already created it. Why would you unless you still don't accept this new way of thinking? And that is all it is. A new way of thinking, just not on a conscious level that you have been used to and more on a higher level that you are yet to see. And if you can't see it then you can't understand it, right?

No, wrong.

Just because you can't see it doesn't mean you can't, or won't, understand it and it certainly doesn't mean that it doesn't really exist. Because believe me it does. And so do a lot more things that we can't consciously think or understand about until we let go of the percolator in our minds.

So do us all a favour. Sack the maid and the CEO. Bring back you, whoever you are, or think you are and start living life like you've never ever lived it before.

Or have you?

Have you really already lived this life in another way on another plane and that's how you know exactly what to expect next? Or are you just creating it moment to moment?

Again, you just won't know, and you'll have to continue to deny the truth or take my word for it, if you carry on living life the way you have been.

Let life happen for you instead of you happening to it. After all if you have already gone out and created everything that you've ever wanted the way you get it doesn't really matter, so why bother interfering in it? Let it come to you. All you have to do is prepare yourself for the influx of abundance in whatever you want that to be, clients, money, love, friendship, happiness, good health. Whatever way you see abundance in your life that is the way you have abundance in your life. And if you don't see any then I definitely would start to open your eyes just a little, if not a lot more, so you can see what lies on your horizon. For believe me it is big. And I can tell you that because I've already seen it.

Happy hunting.

Because unless you do something about the way you see things today then that is what you are going to be doing. You are going to be spending a lot of time hunting and playing hide and seek for the abundance you've created and ways of bringing it into your life. Just let it happen. You haven't let go of control, well not totally just conscious control. The rest is all down to you. The YOU that you can't see, but just because you can't see it doesn't mean that it isn't there. Because you are there, and you are larger than life. You are here, there, and everywhere. And that is definitely one bigger story waiting to be told.

Or is it?

Are my story telling days over and I've just accepted who I am so why can't you?

Or am I destined to keep on telling stories one after the other of my future and others like it?

If I could accept myself as being the whole, then could you? Shall we count to three and do it together?

Okay. One,

Are you ready? Two

No going back now, life will never be the same after this. Three

Oh my God! You've done it. You've accepted yourself for who you really are and now you know why you're here and what you can do about that.

See I told you how easy and short it was. Just one, two, three. Or do you not see yet, and you're still stuck on step one?

I don't know what else I can do or tell you to help you anymore but I'm sure I'll think of something.

Meanwhile why don't you go off and have your own talk with the maid and the CEO that is in your life, be it personal or professional and come back when you want to know a bit more of the truth. Come back when you want to have another piece of the jigsaw puzzle that you call life. And most of all come back after a nice big cup of coffee.

13 THE PUZZLE CALLED LIFE

Okay friends. We're nearing the end and I still feel I should apologise for not having written many stories and leading you here under false pretences. But don't worry because that is the least of your worries. This next bit and after that, will have you worrying all the way to the stars and back unless you take it all with a pinch of salt.

What is with this woman? First she talks of coffee now she talks of salt. She must be crazy!

No I assure you I am not. I have just gone into business mode and am using the words that you would probably use within your corporation. And that's the good thing about being you. You can be anything you want to be.

Yes it's true.

You want to be a scientist and discover new and interesting facts about the world then you can be. You want to be a journalist and report on the world economy or latest tragedy happening then you can. You want to be a medical doctor and save someone's life then you can, not in the way you might think though. You want to be a poet then you can be a great poet if you choose.

And that is what it comes down to. The bottom line. You choose.

Whatever you choose in life you get. If you choose a life of pain and strife then you get it. If you choose a life of pleasure and ease then that's what you end up with.

If you choose to be overweight or have health problems then that is how you are. If you choose to be fit and healthy then you will have that instead.

If you choose for yourself and your work, career, business whatever you touch to be a success, then that is what you get. If you choose a job you hate, a life of misery and no money then you get that too.

Whatever you choose you get.

It doesn't have to be that way though. You can stop choosing.

"Stop choosing; now she's definitely gone mad!"

No, I'm still not mad, zany yes, happy, yes, wealthy, healthy and find it hard to stop smiling, yes. Mad? No. I am guilty of all the above and more although I have no guilt about how I am. I'm me and that's all I can be.

Who are you?

Are you still looking in the wrong places for that missing piece of the puzzle or is it here in front of you once more?

Are you fed up of hearing this or do you realise that you are anything or anyone you choose to be?

You don't have to do anything about it except for let go of choice and let the real you that has been hiding all these years come out and start living the life extraordinaire. And it will be extraordinary. You will live a life like no other of complete abundance and happiness without lifting a finger. Or maybe you will lift a finger occasionally when you know something has to be done. No you won't. Why?

Because everyone else will do it for you. People will be bending over backwards to help you and to get a piece of you. They will continue to want a piece of you until they have realised that they are the missing piece and not you. We all hold our own pieces to our jigsaw puzzle of life, not me, you. Others don't know this and will continue to try to have yours, but your piece won't fit in their puzzle. They have to put their own pieces in at their own time. Rather like you climbing the ladder. When you realise you are there then the best thing you can do is stay there and let others come to you. Don't on any account go back down the ladder to help someone back up or try to carry them. You just jeopardise your own way of being and level of success. People will learn by your example not by you dragging them or telling them how it is. They will see it with their own eyes, and this is more than enough evidence for most.

When you read this book and you hear about me or meet me, then you will know what I am talking about. And if you are already at the top, as you are, then we would have been conversing on these subjects and others for a long time before we do meet in the flesh. (Again that's another book in the making,)

Anyway, for now let's stick with one book at a time. We don't really want you to blow your mind?

Or do we?

Isn't that the missing piece to your puzzle and everyone else's and the only way to get it is to blow your mind. Open your mind up so far that it explodes, and you let in the whole truth and nothing else. Sounds right to me. If I find out how then I'll be sure and let you know. Oh I do know; I've written about it in the last seven books I've done. In fact I've written a step-by-step guide to how to do it in every book including this. And it's simple as one, two, and three. Still you already knew that ad nauseam didn't you? So what is still making you disbelief what I am saying? Do you think there is more, or do you want there to be more?

There isn't. In my book, the simpler the better and you can't get simpler than one, two three. Can you?

Or can you?

Depends if you are the fool or wise man, CEO or maid, woman, or man?

Who did you say you were? Or didn't you? Is the jury still out on that one? Or are you happy to accept that once upon a time you thought you were one or more of those characters? Even sometimes you were all, but today you are none. For now you know the truth and have found your missing piece to your puzzle. Now all that remains is for you to keep the puzzle whole and not let anyone else take borrow or beg a piece from you.

And how do you do that?

As always, read on and find out. Or throw this book away and work it out for yourself. Still, it would be a shame to stop now, considering you are so close to the end and the real truth about who you are, wouldn't it?

Okay, if you're happy to continue then I am. Let's turn the page together. After three

One, Two, Three.

14 THE END IS NIGH

Well done for making it this far. You are getting so used to saying one, two and three, that when it comes to doing it you will be a master at it. Won't you?

No? Are you feeling disappointed at things not going how you expected?

Not only has this book not been about what you thought it would be about but I'm not who I said I was?

What do you mean? You're not who you said you were?

Well, I said I was life. I also said I was the man and the woman and the fool and the wise man and the maid and the CEO and I am none of them, or in fact ever have been.

So who am I?

Confession number three; I don't know.

I think I am all those characters and all of the other characters in my previous books. I think I am a writer, because I write, a fortune-teller and psychic because I know the future and I think I am a mass of energy in a physical body with a physical mind. I think therefore I am. I will never really know what I am until I completely let go of my thoughts and let the truth come in.

Just like you. You can never really know who you are until you stop thinking about who or what you are.

You are who you are, and you are who you are for a reason. Life happens in the way it does to you and with you in it, for a reason. Unless you let go of thought you will never have that true vision. The reason you are who you are and what you should do about it now you know. And that can be applied to all walks of life including the business or company that you are part of.

Until you really do let go of thought the truth will always be in front of you, you just won't be able to see it clearly enough to follow it. You will always end up following another or believing in what someone else has to say instead of what you know is right for you. You will always fall short of the mark and keep on reading stories that probably don't make a lot of sense to you or anyone else, for that matter. You will always be the reader instead of the writer if you don't stop trying to imagine who the writer in you is. Just become the writer, don't question how or why you know who you are. Just be you. Live life as you for you, not for another or in another's way. Live life true to you and no one else and all of your pieces will fit into place for you. You will finally know the truth about you and the end will never be nigh. Life will just keep on going on and on getting even more pleasurable, exciting, joyful, and abundant with every step of the way.

Remember it really is as simple as one, two, and three.

CONCLUSION

That's it from me. Sorry if it wasn't what you expected, but then neither am I.

Sometimes life isn't how you expect it to be and the best way to deal with that is to stop expecting and just know that whatever happens it is always good. After all you really have gone out and created it for yourself.

So, if something doesn't happen the way you planned then don't be upset about it. It just wasn't meant to be. What happens instead definitely was and can take you further to the top than you have ever been before. Stop thinking about it or feeling disappointed and just let it happen. It's going to happen whether you like it or not. And if I were you and I'm not, I would rather have fun finding out the truth than be sat at home scared stiff of finding out what I already know. Wouldn't you?

And if you would, then maybe you need to read another of my books before you can truly give up the ghost of Christmas past. Because that is what you are, simply the ghost of a Christmas long gone. Now it's time to make all of your birthdays come at once. So just let them. You need do no more than fall back into the future that already awaits you and lies just around the next corner of truth for you. Let whatever information or knowledge you have been hiding, about you, enter into your mind. No longer into the coffee pot of time but in straight away and digested and embodied as your truth. So that you can get on with the important things in life of enjoying yourself by living life for you.

Again, and I will say it one last time, nobody knows the truth about you, only you do. No one can walk the three steps to find your answers to your questions only you can. And nobody can or will really live your life for you. That is all down to you.

I hope this has been of use to you. It certainly opened my eyes when I read it as I first wrote it and then eighteen months later as I found out the real reason for writing it. To tell me who I am and not you. And now you can use it to help you find out the truth about you.

Are you ready for a simple life and a profitable enjoyable career? Or do you still hesitate on taking the steps forward in what you need to do? Have you forgotten what those steps are?

Shall I refresh your memory?

Alright then, just this once and no more.

Go on you can do it. Say after me

One, Two, Three.

See I told you that you knew how all along.

And here ends the story of the maid and the CEO.

AUTHOR'S NOTE

Just a little note to tell you that there was no earthquake in San Francisco on Oct 2nd at 11am 2004.

No I didn't lie. No I wasn't mistaken. So what was the point of writing that if I knew it wasn't true?

The point is I was trying too hard to convince you that I could see the future and I realised

- Just because you read or hear something that doesn't mean to say it is true

- Whoever told you to believe everything you read was and never will be me

- Why do you still trust another's words over and above your own?

The only way you can be sure something is true is by feeling it inside of you. Wait until the coffee pot of time has well and truly percolated then you will understand what I mean.

And that is something I will leave you to find out on your own

Goodbye and Thank You.

Love Julie-Ann.

ABOUT THE AUTHOR

From a child Julie-Ann Blackmore knew she could make a difference to the world and focused on health. For over 4 decades she has worked, voluntarily and paid, with many individuals and groups offering her accurate guidance in bringing improvements to their personal and professional health. During this time, she used her Extra Sensory Perception, undertook her own research, trained, qualified in different areas of health and business, and continued to develop herself to understand and effectively master the power of her mind. This enabled her to elevate her methods of working with others creating far more advanced results in their health. As a prolific author, she has self-published a broad range of self-development books. Julie-Ann combines her own words, written and spoken, and art with her unique ability of knowing how her recipient thinks, tailor-making her work to suit each customer's self-development needs. Healing, guiding, enlightening, expanding, inspiring, and developing them as far as they want to go in creating changes in their own health, all areas of life and to realise their own potential as an individual and as part of a bigger whole. She currently lives in Bath and is the founder and MD of How To Be You Ltd. For her works www.howtobeyou.com